Celebrating
INCARNATION

Celebrating INCARNATION

A RESOURCE FOR WORSHIP

Linda McKiernan-Allen, EDITOR

Chalice Press
St. Louis, Missouri

All scripture quotations, unless otherwise indicated, are from the *New Revised Standard Version Bible*, copyright 1989, Division of Christian Education of the National Council of the Churches of Christ in the USA. Used by permission.

The poem "Opposites" is used by permission of author, Judy Gattis Smith. © Judy Gattis Smith.

"Creator, Spirit, Hear Us Sing" by Ann Smith, is used by permission of © Chalice Press.

"Pentecost Prayer" by Michael J. Walker is from *Praise God: A Collection of Resource Material for Christian Worship* by Michael J. Walker, published by The Baptist Union, London, England.

"Wind Who Makes All Winds That Blow" by Thomas H. Troeger is published by Oxford University Press, 200 Madison Avenue, New York, NY 10016. © Oxford University Press.

Cover and interior design: Elizabeth Wright
Cover art: Detail from stained-glass window, Good Shepherd Lutheran
    Church, Minneapolis, Minnesota; photograph © The Crosiers

This book is printed on acid-free, recycled paper.

Visit Chalice Press on the World Wide Web at
www.chalicepress.com

10 9 8 7 6 5 4 3 2 1   99 00 01 02 03

Library of Congress Cataloging–in–Publication Data

McKiernan-Allen, Linda
    Celebrating Incarnation : a resource for worship / by Linda McKiernan-Allen, editor.
        p.   cm.
    ISBN 0-8272-0478-7
    1. Incarnation—Prayer-books and devotions—English.   2. Worship programs. I. McKiernan–Allen, Linda.
BT220.C45 1999
264— dc21   99-050441
                                                                        CIP

Printed in the United States of America

Contents

Preface
vii

List of Contributors
ix

Genesis 1:1—2:4a
Laura Loving
1

Exodus 3:1–12
Christy Bristow
11

1 Samuel 16:1–13
Rebecca Button Prichard
23

Psalm 23
Kadi Billman
33

Psalm 150
Rebecca Button Prichard
43

Isaiah 11:6–9
Linda McKiernan-Allen
53

Matthew 1:18–25
Diana Hagewood Smith
63

Mark 1:1–15
Susanne VanderLugt
71

Luke 10:38—11:4
Peggy McClanahan
81

John 20:1–18
Sharon Thornton
91

Acts 10:1–48
Peggy McDonald
101

Revelation 21:1–7
Laura Loving
111

Music Suggestions: Hymns and Anthems
Bill Thomas
119

List of BIBLE QUEST Scriptures
123

Preface

Throughout the whole of scripture, one of the most important and far-reaching concepts is incarnation. God with us in the flesh, in the form of Jesus Christ, centers the Christian understanding of God-made-known.

God's presence is a vital theme from Genesis to Revelation. Perhaps nothing is more central to worship than a sense of God's presence and activity within human life.

This volume of worship resources provides worship services for twelve different scripture passages that illustrate the range of biblical thinking about incarnation, including Old and New Testament texts. Each chapter provides a call to worship, an opening prayer, a prayer of confession, words of assurance, prayers of the people, a children's sermon, two sermon starters, an offering meditation, an offering prayer, a communion meditation, and a benediction, all based on the scripture text. Some chapters provide additional worship resources for special occasions. The book also provides a chart suggesting hymns and anthems for the theme of incarnation.

These worship services are ideal for congregations that are focusing attention on incarnation during any part of the church year. They can be used sequentially or one at a time. Many of the individual pieces of liturgy could be used as parts of other services, but the use of an entire service can help lend unity to the worship experience.

Many congregations will be using the BIBLE QUEST curriculum, which focuses on the theme of incarnation in the year September 2000 through August 2001. All the bookmark stories from the BIBLE QUEST curriculum are used in this book, and the months of those scriptures can be found in the list of BIBLE QUEST scriptures at the back of the book.

List of Contributors

Kadi Billman lives in Chicago, Illinois. A United Methodist clergywoman, Kadi currently lives her ministry as a participant in a local congregation and as associate professor of pastoral theology and Dean at Lutheran School of Theology at Chicago.

Christy Bristow lives in Hillsboro, Oregon, and is a member of Murray Hills Christian Church (Disciples of Christ) in Beaverton, Oregon. She was educated at Northwest Christian College. She is a published playwright and directed Christian drama in the Seattle area for fourteen years.

Patricia Hatfield, author of the children's sermons, brings both academic preparation and lifelong experience to her work as a Christian educator. A member of the Christian Church (Disciples of Christ), Patricia lives in Indianapolis, Indiana, and works with congregations eager to enliven their education program.

Laura Loving is a United Church of Christ pastor and retreat leader from Waukesha, Wisconsin. Her parish setting is a Presbyterian church, where she practices a shared ministry with the laity. She leads workshops and retreats focusing on everyday spirituality. Recently she co-authored *Celebrating at Home: Prayers and Liturgies for Families*.

Peggy McClanahan is pastor of Pilgrim United Church of Christ in Chicago, Illinois. As a minister within the United Church of Christ, Peggy has pastored in Oklahoma, Iowa, Nebraska, and Illinois.

Peggy McDonald is a Presbyterian Church (USA) minister who has served on the staff of a suburban congregation and a middle judicatory governing body. She is a wife and mother, living in Indianapolis, Indiana.

Linda McKiernan-Allen, ordained in the Christian Church (Disciples of Christ), has served in local pastorates in New Jersey, Nebraska, and Indiana. She has worked in community ministries and at the Regional and General levels of the Christian Church (Disciples of Christ). She has written curriculum and worship resources and is a regular contributor to some worship resource magazines.

Rebecca Button Prichard is a minister of the Presbyterian Church (USA). She has served parishes in Scotland, California, and Indiana. Her Ph.D. in Theology is from the Graduate Theological Union in Berkeley, California. Over the years she has taught worship, church history, and theology at the seminary level. She is presently pastor of Tustin Presbyterian Church, Tustin, California. Rebecca's creative interests include calligraphy, music, and writing. Her book *Sensing the Spirit* was published by Chalice Press.

Diana Hagewood Smith serves the United Methodist Church in Bays Head, New Jersey. A United Methodist clergywoman, she faces the challenges of parenting young children and pastoring a congregation on a daily basis.

Bill Thomas lives in North Hollywood, California, where he works as an actor. An active layman in the Christian Church (Disciples of Christ), he serves as Minister of Music at Church of the Valley Christian Church in Van Nuys, California. A frequent speaker, musician, and keynoter, Bill brings a love of God, a love of the gospel, and an eagerness to utilize his whole being in his vocations.

Sharon Thornton teaches pastoral theology at Pacific School of Religion in Berkeley, California. She is a minister in the United Church of Christ.

Susanne VanderLugt is a minister in the United Church of Canada and lives in Toronto, Ontario. She is a graduate of the Doctor of Ministry in Preaching program at McCormick Theological Seminary.

Genesis 1:1—2:4a

Laura Loving

This service celebrates God's ongoing creativity with echoes from the creation story, mindfulness about the present, and forays into the future.

CALL TO WORSHIP

In the beginning God created the heavens
   and the earth.
The earth was without form and void,
   and darkness was upon the face of the deep;
**and the Spirit of God was moving
   over the face of the waters.**
This is the day that God has made.
Let us rejoice and be glad in it!
Let us worship God.

OPENING PRAYER

Brooding God, hover over us in this time of worship.
Stir in us imagination, courage, reverence,
   awe, indignation, and playfulness.
Shape our unformed yearnings into prayer.
Create from the primordial soup of our dissatisfaction
   a desire to challenge and change the world.
Take us, this wild mix of your people,
   and make of us one people,
      united in our love of justice,

our passion for peace,
and our willingness to take the risk
of continuing the vision you have begun.
Bless us and call us your own.
Amen.

PRAYER OF CONFESSION (UNISON)

O God, Creator of all that is,
we have been poor caretakers of your creation.
We have thought of ourselves first.
We have lived for the moment
and ignored the wisdom of the past
and the fragility of the future.
We confess that we pay more attention
to the things we have created
than to the goodness you provide—
to walls and barriers, which make us feel safe;
to stacks of stocks and storage bins,
which make us feel rich;
to toys and pleasures, which make us feel happy.
Restore in us the knowledge
that our first security is in you.
Remind us of the richness of servant life
lived in answer to Christ's call to discipleship.
Refresh us with the joy of simple things,
of worship, rest, service, and play.
Call us back to the center of our lives,
which is in you,
and help us, in your image, to call that "good."
Amen.

WORDS OF ASSURANCE

God has given us the good life,
a life of forgiveness and mercy.
God has created us and still calls us "good."
We are made new each day through the touch of the
Creator, the love of the Christ,
and the breath of the Spirit.
Thanks be to God for the good news,

which frees us and makes us whole!
Alleluia! Amen.
(*Congregation may sing a response like Taizé "Gloria,"
"Heleyuyan," "Allelu," etc.*)

PRAYERS OF THE PEOPLE

Star-throwing God, you have strewn the heavens
　　with light and wonder.
**We praise you for the star-spangled ceiling of
delight**
　　that arches over us
　　and reminds us how small we are.
Cloud-breathing Holy One,
　　you have cushioned the earth
　　with batting and beauty.
We are grateful for the comfort of your creation.
Water-spilling refresher of our souls,
　　you continue to quench our thirst,
　　to carry us on your tides,
　　to drench our arrogance,
　　to wash away our sin.
We are in awe of your continuing care.
Drafter of all life,
　　you designed the platypus and the porpoise,
　　the aardvark and the whale;
　　you developed the complex human being,
　　tall and small, graying and growing,
　　wondrous to behold.
Make us mindful of life's precious details,
　　the fragile balance of nature,
　　the spectacle of species.
God of past, present, and future,
　　the world is in your hands.
Help us to understand the mysteries of life,
　　to tolerate the ambiguities,
　　to be patient with the mystical,
　　to accept with grace the disappointments,
　　and to remain open to the next chapter.
We pray in hope. Amen.

—or—

Mothering, fathering, embracing, correcting God,
    shape us again and again in your image.
Give us the lofty dreams
    that reflect the height of the firmaments.
Give us the depth of wisdom
    that echoes the deep of the oceans.
Give us the tenderness of touching, discovering,
    and reveling in the bodies you have created.
Give us respect for all creatures, all living things,
    the dark brown earth on which we stand
        and which we pave over, dig up, and defile,
    the pure air that disappears
        like wisps of yesterday's hopes
        to be replaced
        with the residue of our progress.
Gather us up in your arms again, O God.
Cradle us in your hopes and dreams
    and spin us out into the world again
    to start anew,
    to live in you,
    to restore, create, renew, and refresh
        this sagging, sigh-laden planet.
Restore in us deep hope
    and full energy for this calling. Amen.

CHILDREN'S SERMON: BEGINNINGS (BY PATRICIA HATFIELD)

Good morning. Have any of you begun a new year of
school? How many of you have begun school for the very
first time? How many of you are going to a new school this
year? This is also the time when we begin a new year of Sunday school. How many of you came (*or are going*) to Sunday
school this morning? Great! This is a time of new beginnings.

Can you think of other new beginnings we have this time
of year? Have any of you had a new beginning you would
like to share? (*Beginning in a new home, getting new brother or
sister or pet; listen attentively to their responses.*) You've certainly
had a lot of new beginnings! How does it feel to have a new

beginning? (*Affirm whatever feelings the children express.*) New beginnings sure make us feel _____ (*rename the feelings the children mentioned.*)

This morning our Bible story is from the book of Genesis. Did you know Genesis is the very beginning of the Bible? (*Show them a Bible.*) Even the first words of the book of Genesis are "In the beginning." (*Again, show them a Bible.*) Genesis tells us all about the very beginning of the world! In fact, in the Hebrew language the word *Genesis* means beginning. The whole book of Genesis is stories of new beginnings!

From the very first beginning, when God created the world, to the new beginnings each of you have had (*list two or three of the beginnings the children shared*), God is there. God knows beginnings can be scary or exciting, that they might make you feel happy or sad, or all of these feelings all mixed up together! We can always ask God to help when we are beginning something for the very first time. Remember how God blessed the beginning of the world, "God saw everything that he had made, and indeed, it was very good" (Gen. 1:31a)? We want God to bless our beginnings, give us strength and courage to face them, and help us through them. Let's ask God to bless our beginnings right now!

[*Prayer*:] Dear God, thank you for all our new beginnings. Thank you for strength and courage when we try new things. We praise you for always being there for us. In Jesus' name we pray. Amen.

SERMON STARTER: CREATIVITY

Read through the text as poetry, then write down some other images that come to mind that would expand the poetry of the creating God, such as a mother rocking the cradle, humming a lullaby, spilling her love out into the universe; or a lonely creator looking for a companion. Use this expansive imagery to shape your sermon.

Use James Weldon Johnson's "Creation" from *God's Trombones* (New York: Viking Press, 1927, © 1955 by Grace Nail Johnson). Using this poetry, incorporate liturgical dance, music, and the dramatic use of lighting to tell the creation story.

The creative process might be addressed in the grammatical intricacies of the opening section of Genesis. (Cf. Walter Brueggemann, *Texts for Preaching: A Lectionary Commentary Based on the NRSV—Year B* [Louisville: Westminster/John Knox Press, 1993]). One is introduced to two ways of interpreting the beginning of the story. The more familiar translation is "In the beginning, God created...," which gives an absolute new beginning, an artist with a clear canvas. In this translation, verse 2 and its chaos are subordinate. The NRSV rendering takes the first word of the Hebrew text as a temporal, dependent clause: "When God began to create..." and verse 2 is the main clause. The result is the concept of God working with the chaos, ordering and using it. One might wish to look at these two different approaches as different portraits of the artist at work.

Work with the concept of *ruach*, traditionally translated as "Spirit," but more recently translated, including in the NRSV, as "wind." With this image of an unwieldy, artistry-wielding God-force, one could make a case for the messiness of creativity, the risks to be taken as an individual, as a congregation, in shepherding the chaos and receiving the wind of God for change, transformation, cleansing, or renewal. Preaching on the call to creativity within the congregation, use this imagery to grant permission for taking risks! "The wind given by God...blows over the waters and blows them back, making life space dry and safe" (ibid., 98). Perhaps that is the call of the church as well, created in the divine image, called to blow back the swirling waters and make life space dry and safe.

Creativity might also be addressed as a call to mindfulness: Calling people to respond through some art medium, name the different steps of creation: day and night, creeping creatures, the creation of humans; any of these scenarios could be lifted up as a call to pay attention to the world around us. Challenge the listeners to create some work of art to bring back the following week (projects like this are sometimes wasted on the young). Sing us your psalm of creation! Take note of the sunrise and the sunset and read us your poetry!

Paint a menagerie of created beings with watercolors! Punch out a braille haiku that speaks of the awesome act of creation. In short, involve the listeners in the creative process, which echoes the wind of God blowing through the universe.

Focus on Sabbath as an important feature of the Call to Creativity. Note the blessing of Sabbath. Inquire of the text whether this speaks to you as a preacher, needing refreshment. Listen to the text on behalf of the congregation, challenging the business of congregational life and questioning whether creativity is being enhanced or impeded as you keep the spin of meetings and activities (even the order of worship or duties of the church office!). Read the text as a call to Sabbath and see how that intersects with your context of ministry.

SERMON STARTER: STEWARDSHIP AND
ENVIRONMENTAL AWARENESS

Use the passage meditatively to call people to awareness. Use the preaching time to read each segment of the creation, allow time for silence, and incorporate a litany that confesses abuse of the planet, praise for the particulars, or declarations of commitment to continue the restorative functions of people created in God's image.

Deal with the complexities of the call to caretaking. Address the confusion that has existed over the translation of the word dominion (*rada*). (See *New Interpreter's Bible*, vol. 1 [Nashville: Abingdon Press, 1994], 346.) The commentary uses the idea of caretaking as reflecting the way in which God related to the nonhuman. With the touch of the creator, we might lovingly nurture rather than subdue or exploit the earth. Again, the call to recognizing the ways in which we reflect God's image is key. The command to subdue the earth "involves development of the created order. This process offers to the human being the task of intra-creational development, of bringing the world along to its fullest possible creational potential" (ibid.).

Use the stewardship theme as part of ongoing stewardship education. This sermon could contextualize stewardship in the broader context of using the gifts we've been given, caring for the resources entrusted to us, mimicking God's generous spirit.

Focus on particular ways that the congregation could use the inspiration of the creation story to embark on environmental justice ministries. Contact someone from the Sierra Club or Audubon Society or a local legislator working on wetlands preservation to come for the Time for Mission. Ask the youth to comb the newspapers for examples of environmental justice at work and invite them to create a montage of readings and litanies that lift up the encouraging possibilities for action. Create a prayer chain that moves beyond the aches and pains of your members and lifts up the aches and pains of the planet. Emphasize the partnership we have with the God who is still creating, still spinning spiderwebs, dividing cells, and washing the sky with color.

OFFERING MEDITATION

God has showered us with good gifts.
So we respond with this offering of our gifts.
All are not enjoying the riches of creation.
**Some are held hostage by poverty, hunger,
    or homelessness.**
Some are imprisoned by selfishness, hoarding,
    or greed.
**As we offer our gifts, we seek to restore
    the balance of riches
    so that all might enjoy the abundance
    of God's creation.**
Spill out, pour forth, shed your gifts with joy.
**We offer ourselves and our gifts
    with praise and thanksgiving.**

OFFERING PRAYER (UNISON)

**You have given us night and day;
    we offer you the gift of our hours
        for service, prayer, work, worship.
You have created the fruits of the earth;
    we offer you the fruits of our labors.
You have given us the gift of your love**

in your Son, Jesus Christ;
**we offer you the response of our love,
made incarnate in the ministry we perform
in Christ's name.**
**Accept our offerings and bless their use in the
world.**
Amen.

COMMUNION MEDITATION

In the creation story the rhythm of the drama builds from the overture of God's bringing forth form from inchoate darkness to the act of creating humans in God's likeness. And then the sacred rest begins, the breath between acts. The words "it was very good" hang in the air like the delicious aromas emanating from fresh bread and indigo wine.

It is very good to gather here at the hearth of God's creativity, where the hope of the world was kneaded into the one who said, "This is my body, given for you."

It is very good to drink at this table from the deep cup of hope, taking the promise from the One who said, "This cup is the new covenant in my blood."

Here at this table the drama of creation continues, creating an unbroken line from Maker to Redeemer to Comforter.

Here we step onto the stage and take our part in the divine liturgy, taking on Christ's brokenness and generous spilling for all of creation.

Come, taste, and see that the Lord is good.

BENEDICTION

May the Spirit of God carry you from this place;
**May the breath of God fill our nostrils,
    our heads, and our hearts.**
May the Word of God fortify you for the days ahead;
May Christ's life be made new in us and through us.
May the imagination of God
    keep shaping you in the divine image;
**May God create in us clean hearts
    and grant us right spirits for our ministry.**
Go in peace, to love and serve the Lord.
Thanks be to God.

Exodus 3:1–12

Christy Bristow

The Exodus 3:1–12 text tells of God's encounter with Moses on Horeb (sometimes called Sinai—"the mountain of God") through the burning bush. Fire plays a key part in the story, and in worship. (See also Gen. 15:17; Ex. 19:18; Ezek. 1:27 for fire-images of God.)

SETTING THE SCENE

This service would work well for almost any recognition of ministry: Week of the Ministry celebrating pastors, a commitment by the congregation to some new ministry like Habitat for Humanity, or if you have a member who begins seminary and you want to celebrate that decision. It would also work well for Pentecost. In that case, the sermon could go along the lines of "God's Spirit Then and Now." What is God asking this congregation to do today, or how does God communicate with people?

Focusing worship on Exodus 3:1–12 encourages use of a variety of senses to express awe, reverence, and thanksgiving. Fire imagery may emerge in liturgical dance (even in fire dancing), in banners, in massed candles, or in a lit brazier.

Remember to check your storeroom. Do you have Pentecost flame banners or decorations? To make a burning bush, tie torn strips of red and orange cloth to a shrub. Place a battery-operated fan under it to move the torn strips. You could plant the shrub during coffee hour. (Consider Red Chokeberry [*Aronia arbutifolia, cultivar "Brilliantissima"* reportedly

11

has the most brilliantly red fruit], or Winged Spindle Tree [*Euonymus alatus*], also called Burning Bush.)

A pair of worn leather sandals nearby will tell more of the story.

PREPARING FOR THE SERVICE

This service includes visual and spoken cues that work to help worshipers (both leaders and congregation) experience God-made-manifest in the familiar story of Moses at the burning bush.

The first three worship items are very tightly related. The introit (or sung call to worship) states our intention of praying. The invocation and hymn together form the prayer, with "In Jesus' name. Amen." spoken after the hymn. They will be much more effective if you can keep your congregation from stopping between them.

CHORAL CALL TO WORSHIP

> Every time I feel the Spirit moving in my heart,
> I will pray.
> Yes, every time I feel the Spirit moving in my heart,
> I will pray.
> Upon the mountain, my Lord spoke.
> Out his mouth came fire and smoke.
> While God leads me, I'll not fear.
> I am sheltered by God's care.
> Every time I feel the Spirit moving in my heart,
> I will pray.
> Yes, every time I feel the Spirit moving in my heart,
> I will pray.
>
> (*African-American spiritual*)

OPENING PRAYER

> Spirit of God, we have gathered in this place to pray.
> **And to make ourselves ready for your coming.**
> Give us faith,
> **that when you come like the wind,**
> **though we do not see you,**
> **yet we may hear what you are saying to us**
> **and discern your movement.**

Give us courage,
> that we may not fear the tongues of flame:
> **Let all that is unworthy , impure,**
> **and sinful be burned from our lives.**
> **May we know that it is love that burns so brightly**
> **and love that strips away our sin.**

Give us an open mind, Lord,
> that the truth you bring
> may make its home with us:
> **Truth to set us free,**
> **truth to guide us and inform us,**
> **truth to lead us in the way of your will.**

Give us an open heart, Lord,
> that we may seek all people for your realm
> and set no limits to the proclaiming of your word.

Holy Spirit, with the whole church we wait for you,
> in every place and in every generation.

Come, wind.
Come, fire.
Come, truth.
Come, love.

(Incorporate the following hymn into your prayer or use it as a choral response to the prayer.)

Wind who makes all winds that blow—
gusts that bend the saplings low,
gales that heave the sea in waves,
stirrings in the mind's deep caves—
aim your breath with steady power
on your church this day, this hour.
Raise, renew the life we've lost,
Spirit God of Pentecost.

Fire who fuels all fires that burn—
suns around which planets turn,
beacons marking reefs and shoals,
shining truth to guide our souls—
Come to us as once you came;
burst in tongues of sacred flame!
Light and Power, Might and Strength,
fill your church, its breadth and length.

Holy Spirit, Wind and Flame,
move within our mortal frame.
Make our hearts an altar pyre;
kindle them with your own fire.
Breathe and blow upon that blaze
till our lives, our deeds and ways,
speak that tongue, which every land
by your grace shall understand.
In Jesus' name. Amen.

(*Prayer by Michael J. Walker, twentieth century Baptist Minister
Hymn: "Wind Who Makes All Winds That Blow"
Words: Thomas H. Troeger, 1983; copyright: Oxford University Press, 1983
Music: ABERYSTWYTH 77.77D*)

PRAYER OF CONFESSION

God of Abraham, Isaac, and Jacob,
God of Sarah, Miriam, and Ruth,
    we confess we resist changing the direction
    of our lives at your instruction.
We confess we are more interested
in what you can do for us
    than in what we can do for you.
We confess we are not the people you called us to be.
Like the Israelites wandering in the wilderness,
    we make idols out of things in our lives
    and lavish our time and money on them.
We turn from your path
    and fall back into our comfortable old habits.
We long for security,
    even when we know it is not in our best interest.
We are afraid of what you are asking us to do.
Forgive us, we pray, for our misguided action
    and our passive inaction.
Give us the fire of the Holy Spirit
    to refine and purify us,
    to burn away our self-centeredness
    and our false humility,
    so that we may be your holy church,

engaged in your ministry in this place and this time. Amen.

WORDS OF ASSURANCE

"Blessed be the God and Father of our Lord Jesus Christ, who has blessed us in Christ with every spiritual blessing in the heavenly places, just as he chose us in Christ before the foundation of the world to be holy and blameless before him in love…In him we have redemption through his blood, the forgiveness of our trespasses, according to the riches of his grace that he lavished on us…" (Eph. 1:3, 4, 7, 8a).

PRAYERS OF THE PEOPLE

Let us remember the LORD God of fire and smoke,
>   the God who spoke to Moses
>>   through the burning bush;
>   the God who led the Israelites
>>   with a fiery pillar by night
>>   and a cloud of smoke by day;
>   the God whose glory appeared to the Israelites
>>   like a devouring fire upon Mount Horeb.
Let us remember the LORD God
>   "I Am Who I Am Being,"
>   whose fire fell from heaven on the altar
>>   when Elijah prayed
>>   and burned up the offering
>>   and licked up the water;
>   who sent fire from heaven to dedicate the temple
>>   and filled the house of the Lord with glory
>>   so much that the priests could not enter it;
>   who filled Jesus' followers
>>   with the Holy Spirit at Pentecost,
>>   anointing them each with a tongue of fire.
We do remember you, O LORD God.
We remember, and we honor you
>   when we light candles in our sanctuary each
>   Sunday;
We remember you, O LORD,
>   when we see the flash of lightning in the sky;

We remember you, LORD God,
    when, through the marvels of technology,
        we see your far-distant stars and galaxies.
We know your glory is far beyond our
    comprehension.
We know you as a refiner's fire, a light to the nations.
We know you as a still small voice and a solid rock.
We know you because you sent Jesus to walk among
    us and teach us to do justice, to love mercy,
    and to walk humbly with you all our lives.
Help us, we pray,
    to make our lives manifest his ministry
    and to mold our lives as models
    that continue his ministry.
Amen.

CONGREGATIONAL READING OF THE TEXT (EX. 3:1–12)

Leader: Moses was keeping the flock of his father-in-law
           Jethro, the priest of Midian; he led his flock
           beyond the wilderness, and came to Horeb, the
           mountain of God.

Men: There the angel of the LORD appeared to him in a
           flame of fire out of a bush;

Women: he looked, and the bush was blazing, yet it was
           not consumed.

Leader: Then Moses said,

People: **"I must turn aside and look at this great sight,
           and see why the bush is not burned up."**

Leader: When the LORD saw that he had turned aside to
           see, God called to him out of the bush,

People: **"Moses, Moses!"**

Leader: And he said,

People: **"Here I am."**

Leader: Then he said,

People: **"Come no closer! Remove the sandals from your
           feet, for the place on which you are standing is
           holy ground."**

Leader: He said further,

People: **"I am the God of your father, the God of Abraham, the God of Isaac, and the God of Jacob."**

Men: And Moses hid his face,

Women: for he was afraid to look at God.

Leader: Then the LORD said,

People: **"I have observed the misery of my people who are in Egypt;**

Men: I have heard their cry on account of their task-masters. Indeed, I know their sufferings,

Women: and I have come down to deliver them from the Egyptians, and to bring them up out of that land to a good and broad land, a land flowing with milk and honey…

Men: The cry of the Israelites has now come to me;

Women: I have also seen how the Egyptians oppress them.

People: **So come, I will send you to Pharaoh to bring my people, the Israelites, out of Egypt."**

Leader: But Moses said to God,

People: **"Who am I that I should go to Pharaoh, and bring the Israelites out of Egypt?"**

Leader: He said,

People: **"I will be with you; and this shall be the sign for you that it is I who sent you: when you have brought the people out of Egypt, you shall worship God on this mountain."**

CHILDREN'S SERMON: WITH YOU ALWAYS
(BY PATRICIA HATFIELD)

This morning I would like to tell you a story about Moses. One day Moses was taking care of a flock of sheep and goats on the holy mountain of Sinai. While he was there, an angel of the Lord appeared to him, but not like a picture of an angel. Instead, there was a fire in the middle of a bush. Moses saw that the bush was on fire, but it was not burning up. "This is strange! Why isn't the bush burning up? I will go closer and see." So Moses stepped closer. He could see the fire, but the leaves on the bush were still green, and the bark was still fresh.

When God saw Moses coming closer, the Lord called from the middle of the bush, "Moses! Moses!"

Moses answered, "Yes, here I am."

God said, "Do not come any closer. Take off your sandals because you are standing on holy ground. I am the Lord."

So Moses immediately did as he was told. God told how God's special people in Egypt (the Hebrew people) were being treated very, very badly. God had heard them crying, "Save us!"

With Moses' help, God was going to do just that: "Now I am sending you to the king of Egypt so that you can lead my people to freedom."

Moses heard what God wanted him to do loud and clear. But he came up with a whole list of reasons why he couldn't do the job. But each time he thought of an excuse, God came up with a solution. Finally, God just told Moses to stop worrying. God wasn't going to send him to Egypt alone. "I will be with you always," God told him. So Moses said yes, with God's help, he would lead the people out of Egypt to freedom. Together, they did! God helped Moses, and Moses helped God save the Hebrew people from slavery.

When Moses heard his name being called from the burning bush, he knew God was there. And when God told Moses "I will be with you always," he knew God would be there. Today, people come to churches like ours because they know this is a place where God is. People often feel close to God in the church. What can you see in this room, the "sanctuary," that reminds us of God's presence? (*The cross, the Bible, pictures in stained glass windows, candles, communion elements, all the people.*) Yes, all of these things help us to remember that God is with us. Let's pray.

[*Prayer:*] Dear God, we remember how Moses was afraid that he wouldn't be able to do what You had asked him to do. And we remember how happy Moses was when You said, "I will be with you always." Sometimes we have to do hard things, too. Help us to remember that You are with us always. Amen.

SERMON STARTER: WHO ME?

A book title, *A Whack on the Side of the Head*, gives a helpful image. Seems as though the burning bush came as a whack on the side of the head for Moses. Moses was out taking care of business, probably leaving religion to his father-in-law, Jethro, the priest. Moses was so focused on the ordinary, daily, mundane parts of life, God had to whack him on the side of the head.

How can we live our lives in ways that allow us to respond to God's prompting, to take off our shoes and stand on holy ground, to listen *and to change direction* (biblical repentance)? One of the things that helps us live in this wide-awake, expectant state is our church. By regularly attending to God's business, we set ourselves up to respond in faith. Do not lose courage, for even in scripture, few responded immediately in an affirmative way to God's invitation.

Story possibilities:

- Adam's (Gen. 3:8–10) hiding because he felt naked before God.
- Jeremiah's (Jer. 1:6) "I can't do that. I'm only a boy!"

This sermon also needs some women's stories to preach well.

- The brave midwives who saved Moses (Ex. 1:15ff.).
- Queen Esther
- Lydia (Acts 16:11ff.), who started a church in her house (Acts 16:40)
- Mother Teresa

Go back to the text and the story of Moses, who tried to beg off (Ex. 3:11).

Just as these people were hesitant, but did respond to God, what might happen if you were to respond to God's calling in your own life?

Consider telling the story of one of the saints from your congregation (or someone known in your community). When, where, and how did the person hear God's voice? What did he come to understand as the radical demand of God? How has her life changed because of the "holy ground" on which she stood?

SERMON STARTER: SIGNS AND WONDERS

This sermon seeks to draw the contrast between popular religion (what God needs to do for me) and biblical religion (what I need to do for God).

Luke 2:8–12 helps us understand both the wonder and the sign of this story:

> The wonder: the angel appearing
>   with the glory of the Lord.
> The sign: "You will find a baby."
>   (*After* you go to Bethlehem and search.)

Exodus 3:1–12 returns us to the passage for the day, with the same combination of wonder and sign as we discovered in Luke:

> The wonder: the angel appearing
>   in a flame of fire.
> The sign: you will worship on this mountain.
>   (*After* you have single-handedly wrestled
>   the people from superpower Egypt.)
> Folk religion is content with wonders,
>   lifting up the popularity of guardian angels,
>   whose job is to protect "me and mine,"
> rather than biblical angels,
>   who send people on difficult missions
>   and who the Bible describes like Jedi Knights.
> Acknowledge the popularity of the
>   "Footsteps in the Sand" poem
> and the temptation to understand it
> as God's individual promise to take care of me.

As followers of Christ, we recognize that the wonders and the signs within the scriptures are rarely wonders or signs of what we want God to do for us. Rather, we often find within them a challenge to change, to action, to response.

If this sermon comes during Financial Campaign time, speak of the contrast between "offering" as a response to God's gracious action in the world (what I need to do for God) and "offering" as a way to ensure that God will pay special attention to me (what does God need to do for me). How will our financial commitment change if we acknowledge ourselves as keepers of God's goods?

Conclude with an appeal for awareness of God's wonders and signs and a willingness to be Moses-like in our response.

Offering Meditation

Moses managed the flock for Jethro. As Jethro's steward, Moses carried the authority to shepherd the flock. Moses was free to care for the flock as he thought best. Jethro would judge Moses' stewardship when the time came for accounting: How many new lambs were there, how many sheep were lost, how much wool and meat did they produce?

As baptized believers and followers of the Way, we are Jesus' stewards. We come to account for our stewardship every week at this time. With our presence, our tithes, and our offerings, we account for our time and energy. From our ministries of this week, let us put our revenues to work for his ministry.

Offering Prayer

All things come from you, Creator God. We need regular reminding that ultimately we work for you. Bless these returns on your investments. Bless us in our ministries. Guide us in becoming more faithful stewards. In Jesus' name we pray. Amen.

Choral Response

"Here I Am, Lord," no. 452, Chalice Hymnal
Words: Daniel L. Schutte, 1981
Music: HERE I AM, LORD; copyright: Daniel L. Schutte &
New Dawn Music, 1981
(The second verse does not speak directly to the scripture, but the third verse with references to "a feast" with "finest bread" and "giving my life" leads into communion. The tenor line on the chorus makes a lovely soprano descant.)

COMMUNION MEDITATION

In the story of Moses and the burning bush, we sometimes get so caught by the details, we miss the wonder of the story itself. Here is a story of one person's encounter with the Holy! For Moses, it was frightening. He was minding his own (or his father-in-law's) business. Suddenly, he finds he's on God's mountain, and he is afraid to look at God.

When we come to a time of communion, we sometimes get so caught by the details, we miss the wonder of the event itself. Here is an open invitation to all who will come to remember Christ! It is our opportunity to encounter the Holy! And it can be frightening, for there are no masks here. God knows what we will not even admit to ourselves. We are on God's turf, and we could be afraid to look.

Yet at this table, we are beloved guests. Christ has invited all who are followers of the Way to share in the feast. Here we find "a land flowing with milk and honey," for in a simple cup and loaf, there is sustenance and sweetness for our souls.

CHORAL BENEDICTION

Creator, Spirit, hear us sing;
Breathe fire into the praise we bring.
The mighty wind still lives in power;
The church renewed responds this hour.

(Words: Ann Smith, 1989; copyright: Chalice Press
Recommended tune: TALLIS CANON [LM])
Try singing this round a cappella.

1 Samuel 16:1–13

Rebecca Button Prichard

The 1 Samuel text helps a congregation see a biblical precedent for anointing leaders and encourages people to look beyond the outer appearance to recognize one in whom God is at work.

SETTING THE SCENE

This brief narrative about God's choosing and anointing of David follows God's rejection of Saul. It introduces the cycle of narratives that tell of David's rise to power and his reign as king of Israel. The story involves a three-way conversation in which God speaks through Samuel to Jesse and his sons in order to name and anoint David as king. Samuel's role in anointing David with holy oil illustrates well God's appointing and anointing of leaders—of prophets, and priests, and rulers—to perform holy work in the world.

PREPARING FOR THE SERVICE

This text would lend itself well to a service in which congregational leaders or teachers were being recognized, installed, commissioned, or ordained. The use of oil to anoint such leaders might offer the chance to employ an ancient practice in a contemporary setting.

CALL TO WORSHIP

Listen! God's voice calls to us.
We hear God calling.
Look! God will provide for us.

We see God working in our midst.
Come! God is making us holy.
We welcome the Spirit's power.

OPENING PRAYER

God of the prophets, priests, and rulers
who have gone before,
we come into your home having heard your voice.
In every age
you have called your people into community,
welcoming saint and sinner alike
into the household of faith.
Anoint us now with your presence.
Rush into our midst on Spirit wings.
Establish your reign in our hearts.
In the name of the Triune God we pray.
Amen.

A LITANY (OF DEDICATION OR ORDINATION FOR LEADERS OR
TEACHERS IN A CHURCH)

In days of old God called prophets, priests, rulers.
God called them by name, appointing, anointing.
The prophets spoke for God;
they saw things from God's perspective.
The priests served God in worship;
they ministered on behalf of God's people.
Godly rulers provided for the welfare of all;
they led with the common good at heart.
Just so, we appoint and anoint leaders in Christ's
church:
Prophets and preachers and teachers;
Interpreters and sages and visionaries;
Apostles and evangelists and musicians;
[Elders and deacons;
trustees and treasurers;*]
hearing God's call, receiving God's Spirit.
Saints of God, one and all!

**Insert here the offices and titles appropriate to your
particular congregation.*

PRAYER OF CONFESSION

> All-seeing God,
>> you see us as we are, as wayward sheep,
>> well-meaning yet weak,
>> valued and loved yet fearful.
> All-loving God, we are short-sighted,
>> valuing appearances,
>> shallow in our judgments,
>> selective in our neighborliness.
> All-merciful God, forgive and free us,
>> for we long to see with your eyes,
>> to know ourselves and our neighbors
>> through the eyes of love.
> In the name of Christ who sees,
>> who loves,
>> who forgives us all,
>> we pray. Amen.

PRAYERS OF THE PEOPLE

The prayers, focusing on a theme of wholeness, integration, holiness, and wholeheartedness, could move logically from personal to global concerns. The series might naturally begin with prayers for healing of body and soul and of broken personal relationships. Healing of group relations in our nation, race relations, and religious differences could focus on specific cases from the week's news—church burnings, hate crimes, school shootings, domestic violence. International peace, the healing of creation, and prayers for reconciliation among tribes and nations and enemies would seem a natural progression from prayers for wholeness and healing in personal, interpersonal, and natural spheres. Language of anointing and healing, of shalom, and of a reign of peace would resonate well with the language of the scripture lesson.

CHILDREN'S SERMON: A NEW KING (BY PATRICIA HATFIELD)

Can anyone tell me what a king is? (*Listen to the children's answers.*) Yes, a king is a leader or someone who is in charge of a country. Do you know what a king does? (*Makes laws; leads the army; speaks for the people.*)

So what do you think a king looks like? (*Old or young; tall and strong; wears a purple robe and crown.*) Someone who looks like that we expect would surely be a strong and powerful king, able to lead the people in war and in peace.

In our Bible story today, we hear how God chooses a new king for the Hebrew people. God tells the priest, Samuel, to go to Jesse, a father with eight sons. The Lord would tell Samuel which one of the eight boys would be the new king. When Samuel arrived at Jesse's house, he saw the oldest son, Eliab. Eliab was very tall and handsome. Samuel was sure this was the son who would be the new king.

But God said to Samuel, "Don't pay attention to how tall and handsome he is. I have not chosen this son because I do not judge by how a man looks on the outside. I look at the heart."

One by one, Jesse brought seven of his sons before Samuel, but each time Samuel said, "No, the Lord hasn't chosen him. Do you have any more sons?"

Jesse answered, "There is still the youngest, but he is out taking care of the sheep."

"Tell him to come here," Samuel said. So Jesse sent for him. He was a handsome, healthy young man, and his eyes sparkled.

The Lord said to Samuel, "This is the one!"

And right in front of the older brothers, Samuel marked David with special olive oil to show that he would be the new king.

Did you expect God to choose the youngest son to be king? It doesn't matter to God how old we are, or how tall we are, or what we look like. We can still be a king for God if we have a good heart. Do you think there are any kings here today in our congregation? (*Children will probably think this is funny. Mention some of the church leaders such as Sunday school teachers, the board moderator, or the elders.*) All these people were called by God to be leaders in our church, to make rules for our church, and to speak for the people of the church.

Do any of you think that you will be called by God to be a leader in our church? Probably David didn't expect to be chosen. Perhaps some of our leaders didn't expect to be chosen either. But they are serving God through their good hearts and by what they are willing to do. Let's pray:

[*Prayer:*] Dear God, we thank you that you choose leaders by the kind of heart that they have. Help us to have good hearts, to learn about you everyday, and to grow to be the kind of person you want us to be. Amen.

SERMON STARTER: THE LEAST LIKELY

In ancient Israel, priests, prophets, and kings were anointed with oil as a holy sign of their call from God. The holy oil sanctified these chosen servants, giving them a special authority. In this story Samuel plays both a priestly and a prophetic role in the anointing of David. Priests used holy oil to set apart people, places, and things for God's purposes. Priests offered sacrifices to God for the people. Samuel does both these things in this story. Yet Samuel is a prophet, speaking on behalf of God. Samuel, a seer who sees with God's eyes, reveals God's election of David as future king.

The fairytale nature of this narrative strikes us. God speaks through Samuel, carrying on a conversation with Jesse through him. The sons of Jesse, beginning with the eldest, are paraded past Samuel and God and one by one are rejected. The repetition sets up a pattern that leads to the story's climax. The youngest, smallest, most insignificant brother is off tending sheep and must be called in for consideration. The surprise ending to the story is that God chooses the least likely brother for the greatest honor. A sermon based on this passage might focus on God's calling of mere mortals for divine work.

Other familiar passages of scripture resonate with this theme and might easily be brought to bear. The shepherd boy David is anointed king of Israel, so passages employing the shepherd motif might help interpret this passage. "The LORD is my shepherd…[he] anoint[s] my head with oil" (Ps. 23:1a, 5b). When people question or doubt our leadership, it can be comforting to remember God's holy call in our lives. Jesus' parable of the lost sheep and the shepherd who will go to any lengths to seek the stray (Lk. 15:3–7; Mt. 18:12–14) underlines the faithful love of God that reaches out in ways that surprise us. Gospel themes such as "the first shall be last, the last first" are also supported by this story, in which God chooses not the oldest and tallest, but the youngest and least of the brothers.

Perhaps the parade of brothers reminds us of fairy tales in which some sort of choosing takes place. Cinderella, a young and seemingly insignificant girl, is chosen against all odds. The proud father Jesse and his lineup of sons might remind us of the ambitious stepmother and the stepsisters who try in vain to squeeze their feet into the glass slipper. We are as sure that Cinderella's foot will fit as we are that David's boyish charms will fit with God's plans. A powerful point of this story is that if God can call David, God can call us. God's choosing is often of the unlikely.

David was viewed by the Hebrew people as a great king, though we know he was fallible and flawed. Bethlehem is the birthplace of Perez, Obed, Jesse, and David. Jesus' birth in Bethlehem and his Davidic lineage give credence to his anointing as a ruler. Jesus is often spoken of as "prophet, priest, and king," the three roles that required anointing in Israel. A sermon that wanted to draw comparisons between David and Jesus as God's anointed or as shepherds of God's flock would need to be careful not to fall into anti-Judaism. Common points between the two, which carry forward the theme of "the least likely," include Jesus' humble birth, his coming as a child, his anointing to preach good news to the poor, and the crown of thorns.

SERMON STARTER: NOW I SEE

This passage and its narrative structure play upon various ways of "seeing." Samuel is a prophet, a "seer," one who is allowed to see as God sees. The story is framed by Samuel's coming and going, sent by God, carrying his horn of oil, and using it to anoint David as king. In verse 1, God says, "I will provide" a king, but the word translated *provide* is a form of the word *to see*, meaning something like "I will look out for a king," "I will see," or "find a king here," among Jesse's sons. The same Hebrew root is used later to speak of both seeing and appearance. In the pivotal verse (v. 7), Samuel is told not to regard Eliab's "looks." "The LORD does not see as mortals see." Humans see the eyes (the appearance), but God sees the heart.

The way God sees and the way humans see are two different things. When David is finally chosen, it does seem that his appearance matters. He is ruddy, earthy (something like Adam), and his eyes (his appearance) look good. The ambiguity and the irony are probably important. David isn't what Samuel or Jesse or any of us might expect in a king, yet he is exactly what God is looking for.

Eyes, or looks, are compared with heart. Often this verse is seen as an argument for a dualistic view of human nature—we look on the "outer," God looks on the "inner." This view is not supported by the language or by a Hebrew view of human nature. The heart and the body are in unity; the eyes and the heart are connected. Human sight is limited compared with God's insight. What humans value in a leader isn't exactly the same as what God values. David's beautiful eyes and his ruddy appearance suggest that God's vision goes deeper than even Jesse's or Samuel's.

The heart is the center of desire and feeling and intent. This wholeness of heart and soul and body explains why the love of God is to be heart, soul, might (Deut. 6:5). This wholeheartedness reminds us of Jesus' words, "there is nothing outside a person that by going in can defile, but the things that come out are what defile" (Mk. 7:15). Holiness, for Jesus the Jew and for Hebrew scripture, is a wholeness, a wholeheartedness, in which the heart is the center of all affections.

Our age wants to reconnect with this wholeness, this wholeheartedness, this holiness. It is easy to think of examples in our culture and in our world in which humans fail to see as God sees, looking upon human beings as appearance only and not as deeper, integrated reality—from the beautiful people of show business to the hard bodies of athletes. We might also think of ways that dualism comes into play, demeaning outward or physical or material reality that is part of our wholeness in God—racism, ageism, sexism, discounting of persons with any kind of disability. It is comforting and central to our faith to know that God sees us and loves us as whole human beings, that our worth as persons is derived ultimately from God's creative love.

OFFERING MEDITATION

The oil of anointing was a precious commodity. It was given to God by the people of God, along with other valuable gifts, for the worship of God. God's people set aside, sanctified, offered to God a portion of their earthly goods so that the service of God, temple worship, and communal caring could be maintained. The holy oil was used to sanctify, to consecrate, to make people, places, and things holy for the service of God.

Just so our income is a precious commodity. It is a valuable gift of God for our health and well-being and pleasure. As God's people have in all times offered their gifts and sanctified a portion of their wealth, setting it aside for holy use, so we bring what is of value to us and give a part of it to God, setting it apart for the service of God, for the building of community, for a holy anointing of God's world. Let us give to God a gift that costs us something; let us give it freely in thanksgiving and gratitude.

OFFERING PRAYER

God of the ages, you have called us by name; you have made us holy; you have blessed us with gifts both earthly and spiritual. We give to you now of our earthly gifts, and in giving we pledge also our spiritual gifts to your service. As your holy people may we offer your holiness, your wholeness, your healing to a heartbroken world. We pray in the name of the one God: Spirit, Savior, Creator. Amen.

COMMUNION MEDITATION

The elders of the city saw Samuel coming and asked, "Do you come in peace?"

"Peacefully, I come," Samuel replied.

Just so, from one clan to another, from one tribe to another, from one nation to another come the negotiators, the reconcilers, the mediators.

"Do you come in peace?"
asks the Indian chief of the settler;
"Do you come in peace?"
asks the Arab of the Jew,
"Do you come in peace?"
asks the Catholic of the Protestant,
the Bosnian of the Serb,
the Tibetan of the Chinese,
the child of the parent, the wife of the husband...

Into the midst of enmity, adversity, and mistrust, into the midst of a family's power struggle, the prophet, sent by God, comes with the word *Shalom*, Peace.

Just so, Jesus came. Just so, Jesus comes now. Jesus—the prophet, the high priest, the savior—comes into a world of fear and strife, of dissension, of broken relations. Jesus comes saying, "Peace, my peace, real peace, God's peace, I bring."

This bread, this cup (the lifeblood, the body broken) become a peace offering from God to put things right, to put us at rest, to put an end to the hostility. This meal is the shalom, the reconciliation of God in Christ.

Do you come in peace? Christ bids you come. Leave behind your animosity, your anxiety, your fears, your strife. Come in peace, make peace with one another, with God, with yourselves. Come in peace, for Christ, our peace, invites us all.

PRAYER AFTER COMMUNION

God of peace, at this holy meal
we have tasted your shalom.
Christ's death has put to rest our deepest fears,
healed our deepest rifts.
As those at peace with God and one another,
may we now take part in the restoration,
the re-creation,
the reconciliation of the world.

In the power of the Spirit, we pray. Amen.

BENEDICTION

You are people chosen by God,
   a royal priesthood,
   holy each and every one.
Go now in the peace of Christ
   and the mighty power of the Spirit. Amen.

Psalm 23

Kadi Billman

CALL TO WORSHIP

Like the deer that yearns for running streams,
my soul is thirsting for the living God.
We come to praise the living God,
> **who leads the weary beside restful waters,**
> who spreads a table for us,
> **and fills our empty cups to overflowing.**
(from Ps. 42:1–2 and Ps. 23:2, 5)

OPENING PRAYER (UNISON)

**Good Shepherd, thank you for gathering us
together.**
**Lead us more deeply into the mystery
of your companionship.**
Draw us more closely to you and to one another.
**May the refreshment offered here strengthen us
to follow you into a thirsty world. Amen.**

PRAYER OF CONFESSION

God of the still waters and shadowed valley,
> we confess the many ways
> we break trust with you.
When we are so driven by our wants
> that we confuse what we want
> with what we need,
> forgive us and guide us to right paths.

33

When our hunger for comfort and refreshment
    becomes an unending search
    for entertainment
    and escape,
    forgive us and lead us
    to the waters that truly heal and satisfy.
When we seek relief from our fears in activities
    that keep us from truly facing the deep valley,
    forgive us and help us to cling to you
    as our only true security and source of courage.
    For the refuge you are,
    we offer our thanks.
    For the grace to rely on you more deeply,
    we ask your help.
We pray in the name of Jesus.
Amen.

WORDS OF ASSURANCE

"For thus says the Lord GOD: I myself will search for my sheep, and will seek them out. I will rescue them from all the places to which they have been scattered. I will bring them out from the peoples and gather them. I will feed them… with good pasture…they shall lie down in good grazing land. I myself will be the shepherd of my sheep (selections from Ezek. 34:11–15).

PRAYERS OF THE PEOPLE

Holy God, thank you for every tender mercy. For times of renewal and rest, for strength in times of loneliness and exile, for every experience of being gathered to you and gathered with those who embody your loving-kindness, we thank you and praise your name.

God of mercy,

hear our prayer.

We pray for all who yearn for a place of rest and peace, a place that is home. May your church be a haven for longing hearts, and a home for the homeless.

God of mercy,

hear our prayer.

We pray for all who are ill in body, mind, or spirit. May your strength always be found in homes and hospital rooms, in prisons and psychiatric wards, wherever there is need for comfort and companionship in the valley of pain. We lift before you, silently and aloud, the names of those whose needs are known to us (*allow time for names to be spoken silently and aloud*) even as we call on your aid for those whose names are unknown to us.

God of mercy,

hear our prayer.

We pray for all whose lives are shattered by violence on the streets and in their homes. We pray especially for children and remember your promise to carry the lambs in your arms and lead those who are pregnant. May your church be a sanctuary for the vulnerable; a place of restful waters for those who have been violated; a place where people need fear no evil, for you are with us.

God of mercy,

hear our prayer.

We pray for all leaders of all nations. Guide our country's leaders and help them to guide us in paths of righteousness and peace. May your church be empowered to embody your justice and your love in every nation.

God of mercy,

hear our prayer.

We pray for all who grieve, especially for those we name silently or aloud before you now (*leave time for names to be shared silently and aloud*).

Bind up the brokenhearted. Be merciful to those who dwell in the valley of the shadow of death.

Enable your church to be strong enough to hear and to express the laments of those who are suffering. Give us courage to face our pain and grace to remember "you are with me; your rod and your staff—they comfort me."

God of mercy,

hear our prayer.

Into your hands we commend all for whom we pray, trusting in your mercy through Jesus Christ our Lord.

Amen.

CHILDREN'S SERMON: LOVING CARE (BY PATRICIA HATFIELD)

Do any of you have a pet? What are some things you have to do to take care of your pet? (*Provide food, water, and perhaps shelter; some may take pets for a walk—and carry a scoop to clean up after the pet—and keep the place where they live clean* [*fish tank, hamster cage*]). What happens when your pet is injured or sick? (*They may take the pet to a veterinarian and may even take time off work or school to care for the pet.*) And what would you do if your pet were lost? (*Search the neighborhood calling for the pet, put up "lost pet" posters; the children may remember being sad and crying or not being able to sleep until the pet is found.*) It sounds like many of you do lots of different things to make sure your pets are loved and cared for. I have even seen news stories of pet owners calling the fire department to come with their big ladders to rescue a kitten from a tall tree! (*If you have pets, speak specifically about your loving "shepherding" of those animals.*)

This morning, we have another psalm for our Bible story: Psalm 23. It is the most famous psalm of all. Many people know this psalm by heart because knowing it and saying it makes many, many people feel better when they are in times of trouble. Some people call this psalm the *shepherd's psalm* because the person who wrote the psalm tells us God is like a shepherd who cares for a great flock of sheep. A shepherd cares for sheep just like you and I care for our pets.

(*Read verses 1–4 of Psalm 23; after each line or phrase, relate the line to the items the children mentioned they would do to care for a pet: verses 1–2a food; verse 2b water; verse 3 walks with us; verse 4 lost pet; omit verse 5 as we are not exploring banquet imagery here; verse 6 that God will love us and keep us forever.*) Let's pray:

[*Prayer:*] Dear God, thank you for pets to love and care for. We praise you for loving us and caring for us as though we were sheep of a loving shepherd. Help us always to take care of our pets and to remember that you will always take care of us. Amen.

SERMON STARTER: SHEPHERD AND HOST

Psalm 23 gives two images for God: shepherd and host. God is portrayed "as the good Shepherd who cares for the flock…[and] the Host who offers hospitality to a guest and protects the guest from enemies" (Bernhard W. Anderson, *Out of the Depths: The Psalms Speak for Us Today* [Philadelphia: Westminster Press, 1983], 207). In wrestling with the connection between those two images, Bernhard Anderson writes that a shepherd's life involves not only protecting the sheep as they wander, but protecting the traveler, who finds hospitality in the shepherd's tent from dangers and enemies in the desert (ibid., 208).

Both dimensions of care are present in the Jesus stories. In John's gospel, Jesus is the good shepherd whose voice is known and trusted (Jn. 10:1–16). The shepherd also goes out to search for the one sheep that is lost in the wilderness (Lk. 15:3–7). Jesus is also portrayed as the host at the table, both at the Last Supper and in the resurrection stories in which he becomes known to the disciples "in the breaking of bread" (see esp. Lk. 24:28–35). In Luke's account of the Last Supper, Jesus speaks of eating Passover in the kingdom of God (Lk. 22:16). This image of eating and drinking in the world to come is evoked when we call the eucharist "a foretaste of the feast to come."

These images have also been used as images for Christian leadership, especially that of the pastor. (The term *pastoral care* has its origins in the shepherd image.) The worship leader is sometimes called the "presider," and one of the chief joys of ordination in many Christian denominations is the joy of presiding at holy communion.

One of the greatest pressures church leaders experience is the pressure to say the "right" thing, to provide a helpful "solution" to a problem shared, or to lift a heavy burden of sorrow from someone's shoulders. Occasionally, some presiders become loath to share the privileges of distributing communion, or to invite their "flock" into worship leadership, perhaps unconsciously seeing these as benefits for withstanding the pressures of being pastor.

A sermon might wrestle with both the beauty and danger of these realities of ministry. Psalm 23 claims *one* shepherd: Yahweh (or "the Lord"). Even in the Jesus narratives, Jesus is lamb as well as shepherd, guest as well as host. Ministry that follows his example moves between the poles of being

able to offer *and* receive hospitality and care, to be coura-
geous *and* cautious, strong *and* vulnerable.

In essence, Psalm 23 offers a corrective. For caregivers,
the God portrayed in this psalm is not imagined as one who
airlifts persons *over* the valley of the shadow or who leads a
person *out* of the valley. The text simply says that in the valley the sufferer fears no evil because "you are *with* me." God
is imaged here as a *companion* rather than a problem-solver.

And as both companion and host, God provides for the
vulnerable one to be "anointed with oil" and comforted by
"your rod and your staff" (symbols of God's help and pro-
tection, not the Psalmist's own strength).

Conclude with a story that shows ways both "followers"
and church leadership can recognize God as the shepherd
and host. All within the church (including leaders who provide nurture and care within the congregation) are grateful
recipients of God's shepherding attention.

SERMON STARTER: A PSALM OF ORIENTATION

Walter Brueggemann has suggested that one way to look
at the Psalter as a whole is to look at the way the psalms
functioned in the life of the community. In a provocative es-
say titled "The Psalms and the Life of Faith," Brueggemann
suggests three ways the psalms functioned in the life of Israel—to express orientation, disorientation, and reorientation (Walter Brueggemann, "The Psalms and the Life of
Faith," in *The Psalms and the Life of Faith*, ed. Patrick D. Miller
[Minneapolis: Fortress Press, 1995], 3–32).

The psalms of orientation give voice to the community's
sense of being at home in the world, secure and confident.
Many of these kinds of psalms are in the Psalter: in creation
psalms like Psalm 104, which reflect the coherence and goodness of creation; in the psalms that teach clear, reliable retri-
bution, in which evil is punished and good rewarded (e.g.,
1, 119); in some of the psalms of ascent that reflect domestic
life in good order (e.g., 127, 128, 131, 133). These psalms voice
genuine gratitude for rich blessings and portray a world that
is balanced, ordered, and secure (ibid., 10–11).

The psalms of disorientation, the lament psalms, give voice to a shattered reality, an experience of disequilibrium and extremity. Brueggemann suggests that if these laments are about *losing* orientation, then it must be assumed that the lamenter at one time *did* feel at home in the world and is now in a world profoundly unfamiliar. These psalms not only release extreme emotions, but bring to full expression the collapse of the "old orientation," which is not adequate for new circumstances of life. It is necessary to let go of an old world in order to receive a new one (ibid., 21). As Brueggemann has argued in other works as well, "Only grief permits newness." (Walter Brueggemann, *The Hopeful Imagination: Prophetic Voices in Exile* [Philadelphia: Fortress Press, 1986], 9–47.)

Psalms of reorientation are songs "sung at the appearance of a new reality, new creation, new harmony, new reliability" (Brueggemann, 1995, 22). In New Testament terms, resurrection hope is different from hope before the cross. These are songs of scattering and gathering, exile and homecoming. Like sheep without a shepherd (Ezek. 34:5; Mk. 6:34), our lives are often scattered and fragmented; lament best expresses this condition. Yet we may also know seasons of experiencing new consolidation and wholeness, "when the shepherd is with the flock" (Ps. 23:1; Jn. 10:10–11) (ibid., 31–32).

Psalm 23 follows on the heels of one of the Psalter's most powerful psalms of lament, whose opening cry, "My God, my God, why have you forsaken me?" was uttered by Jesus himself at his crucifixion, according to Matthew's and Mark's gospels. A sermon might focus on Psalm 23 in terms of its connection to Psalm 22, dwelling on the experience of trust that comes *within* the deep valley. Psalms like Psalm 23 mirror resurrection hope in the sense that the hope and trust expressed is not naive or blind to the forces of death and destruction. The psalmist is wide awake to danger and enemies. Yet the psalmist remembers and testifies to the God who is trustworthy precisely in that place. The Communion Meditation (*see below*) has this exegetical focus.

OFFERING MEDITATION

Jesus taught us that everything matters: a cup of cold water, a few loaves, a few fish. The mystery of our faith dawns when we offer what we have to Jesus and find it is enough to be of use to God's people. Sometimes our baskets and cups even overflow. Let our gifts be gathered now.

OFFERING PRAYER

Receive what we have gathered, O God, not only these tangible signs of our love, but every gift of service we offer you now in the stillness of our souls [*brief silence*].

Bless all these gifts, and lead us in the paths of grace, justice, and generosity.

In the name of Jesus, our guide and friend. Amen.

COMMUNION MEDITATION

The movie *Places in the Heart* begins with two tragic deaths, a white sheriff shot accidentally by an African-American man, and that of the African-American, quickly killed in return without benefit of trial.

The story refocuses on the sheriff's widow and children, who now must contend not only with grief, but with the loss of their only income. A town banker offers to "help" the widow by purchasing the family land, land she does not want to sell. Then a migrant African-American laborer, who has nothing in life but his strength and wisdom about planting cotton, offers to work the land. Out of mutual need they forge a friendship and work the land until it yields a hard-won, abundant crop.

The partnership between widow and migrant worker is finally torn asunder by the violence of the Ku Klux Klan. The abundant crop enables the widow to keep her land, but the one who gave his sweat and blood to make it flourish is not there to reap a just reward. In the closing scene of the movie the widow is sitting in church. Others are there too, those whose struggles we have watched throughout the film—sinners and sinned against, enemies and friends.

Then a surprising thing happens. As the camera makes a slow, final sweep over the communion scene, we see not only the banker and klansmen, blind man and widow, estranged husband and wife who are the surviving enemies, the surviving friends. We also see the dead—the sheriff and the man who shot him, the migrant worker—seated in the church among the living, taking the bread and lifting the cup. No one in the scene reacts to their presence; the focus stays on passing the bread and cup.

Nothing has changed, in one sense. The filmmaker has given us not the typical Hollywood ending, in which all antagonisms have been resolved and clear justice has been done. The valley of the shadow is still real for all the characters, who grope, still, for dignity. Still present is the struggle to eke out a living, the power of hatred and greed, an unfulfilled justice, the pangs of grief and regret. The dead are still dead.

Yet in another sense, everything has changed. Through the imaginative vision of the storyteller, what is invisible has been rendered visible for a fleeting moment. We catch sight of the human and divine bond that carries our stories from generation to generation and binds us together. We glimpse, just for a moment, the depth of hope and trust that lies at the heart of the Twenty-third Psalm. It is *precisely* amidst what is most broken, what is most impossibly "fixed," that God prepares a table. Here, the deepest reality of what *is* and the deepest assurance of what is *promised* intersect. At God's table no one is left out. No one who hungers and thirsts for bread and hope will be harmed or left with an empty cup.

The Lord prepares a table. Surely our cup overflows. When you have tasted of what is promised, know assuredly, you have been given a foretaste of the feast to come. Amen.

BENEDICTION

> May you go forth strengthened and refreshed
>   by the table, which the Lord prepares.
> May the Spirit of the Risen Christ restore your soul,
>   and may your lives move ever on right paths.
> May you know God's presence in every valley,
>   **and may the grace of our Lord Jesus Christ,**
>   **the love of God,**
>   **and the communion of the Holy Spirit,**
>   **be with us all.**
>   **Amen.**

Psalm 150

Rebecca Button Prichard

SETTING THE SCENE

Psalm 150 is the "doxology" of the Psalter. It culminates and sums up the prayer book used in the worship of ancient Israel, in which the last five psalms (146–150) focus on exuberant praise.

This final psalm calls for praise in all creation, by all creation, and in all kinds of creative modes. This psalm, with its command to employ all types of instruments together with singing and dancing and shouting, invites us to worship in ways that break out of our normal patterns. A service with Psalm 150 as its focus is a perfect occasion to bring arts (dance, instruments—guitars, tambourines, drums, and cymbals—and music that involves movement and clapping) into the order of worship. As the sermon says, "Go crazy!"

PREPARATION FOR THE SERVICE

Make available musical instruments (rhythm band, chimes, bells) for individuals to use during worship. Incorporate their use into the children's sermon and the anthem, along with the hymns. Ask the choir (or another group) to participate with the instruments during the Call to Worship, the Litany and/or the reading of Psalm 150.

CALL TO WORSHIP

Hallelujah!
Praise! Praise God!

We come into God's glorious presence! Rejoice!
We come with all we are and have! Hallelujah!
We come with singing and shouting and dancing!
Hallelujah!
We come as living, breathing souls loved by God!
Praise! Praise God!
Shout for joy!
Hallelujah!

OPENING PRAYER

Great God, Gracious God, Glorious God:
We come to worship, to praise you,
  animated by the very breath of life
  you have given us.
As you breathe your Spirit into all creation,
  so may we live and move
  and have our being in you.
May our worship sparkle with your creativity,
  and may we, in this moment,
  know anew your redeeming,
  forgiving love in Christ,
for it is in Christ's name we pray. Amen.

A LITANY

Praise God!
Where are we to praise God?
In the holy places, in heaven and in earth,
  everywhere!
Why are we to praise God?
For God's mighty might, God's great greatness,
  God's very muchness!
How are we to praise God?
With exuberance and abandon: blowing horns,
  plucking strings!
In whirling dance, shaking timbrels!
With strings and pipes, with shouting and clapping!
With tingling, clashing cymbals!
With crashing cymbals and a shout of joy!
Who is to join in this praise of God?

All living, breathing creatures!
Everyone! Everywhere! Every way we can!
Hallelujah! Praise God!

PRAYER OF CONFESSION

Great God, high and holy, mighty in mercy,
 even as we seek to honor and glorify you
 in our worship,
  we become aware of our weakness and our
  timidity.
We are wholehearted in our enjoyment
 of life and its pleasures,
  yet we spend this hour in caution
  and in quiet boredom.
We engage in work and play with all we are and have,
 yet we offer you, the creator of the universe,
 the lover of our souls,
  only the leftovers of our lives.
Forgive us and make us new, for Christ's sake. Amen.

WORDS OF ASSURANCE

Because we are forgiven creatures of a loving God,
 in this hour, God may
 charge us with the Spirit's power,
 energize us with God's living Word,
 unleash God's divine creativity in us.
Rejoice, and believe you are forgiven,
 that you may live to praise God!

PRAYERS OF THE PEOPLE

Prayers set in the context of this psalm might move from praise and adoration of God's very being to thanksgiving and wonder at creation to a focus on human creation and creativity. The mirror imagery of the second sermon could be employed to move from adoration to thanksgiving to intercession on behalf of God's world. God's glory and greatness must reach to the sick and the suffering, to the sad and sorrowing. Prayer must refocus us, reminding us of our part in reflecting God's mighty mercy where it is most needed.

CHILDREN'S SERMON: A JOYFUL NOISE (BY PATRICIA HATFIELD)

Preparation: rhythm instruments, one for each child.

Our Bible story this morning is not really a Bible story at all: It's called a *psalm*. A psalm is like a poem. The Hebrew people would sometimes say a psalm like a prayer or sing a psalm like a hymn. In the Hebrew language the word *psalm* means praise. Our psalm this morning is called "Praise the Lord!" It is the very last psalm in our Bible and is one of the happiest psalms of all! It's a very happy psalm because the Hebrew people love God and are thankful for all the great things that God has done for them.

The Hebrew people wanted to praise God for helping Noah build the ark and save all the animals. They were thankful that God sent Moses to lead the people from Egypt to freedom. I like to praise God too! (*List two or three things for which you praise God. Don't forget to mention you are thankful you could talk with the children about God at church!*) What would you praise God for? (*The children may need prompting; suggest families, teachers who help them to learn, a safe and clean place to gather.*)

In our psalm the Hebrew people praised God with musical instruments. I'd like us to do that this morning. When I give each one of you a musical instrument, please hold it quietly in your lap. Then I'll read the psalm one line at a time. At the end of each line, I will raise my hand (*demonstrate raising your hand*). That will be the signal for you to play your instrument. When I lower my hand (*demonstrate*), you stop and I will read the next line. Let's practice. (*Say, "Praise the Lord!"; then raise your hand, hold it for a few seconds, and then lower it. You may need to remind the children to stop when you lower your hand so everyone can hear the words of praise. Then read the psalm from your Bible line by line. With the last line, you might want to raise both hands for a big finale of praise!*)

Do you think God liked our praise? Hold your instruments very quietly for a moment so we can pray:

[*Prayer:*] Dear God, we are so happy that you are our God! You have done so many good things. We want to praise you with words and with music. We pray you will accept our praise and help us to continue praising you with our hands, our voices, our minds, and our hearts. Amen.

(*If the children leave the sanctuary for children's church at this time, they might play their instruments as they march from the sanctuary to their classroom.*)

SERMON STARTER BACKGROUND

The central word of this psalm, "praise" or *hallelu*, is repeated over and over again. Short, sweet, and rhythmic phrases abound. *Hallelujah* (Praise "jah," God) is a rich word with layers of meaning: be boastful; brag about God; offer sheer, unadulterated praise to this God. Shout for joy; rejoice; sing as if it were a wedding; worship; shout acclamations, thanksgivings; glorify; bask in God's glory. There is even a link linguistically with madness; go crazy as you celebrate God's splendor and renown. This is done in the temple, in the church, in the place of worship. It isn't a secret. It is proclamation as well as praise, for it is boasting about God's mighty might and great greatness.

The first verse gives praise a location: in the holy place, in holiness, in the temple, in the mighty expanse, in the great firmament, in the expansive heavens, literally everywhere.

The second verse gives praise a reason: for God's sheer greatness, might, valor, God's exceeding greatness ("that than which nothing greater can be imagined"—Anselm). Might and greatness sometimes have a militaristic overtone in scripture, but here they seem to be poetic, parallel, intense statements about God's very being: greatness, might, muchness, strength.

The third, fourth, and fifth verses tell us how, giving us concrete ways to praise God. Most are taken from secular, sensuous merriment and gladness. The list includes a trumpet blast (shofar—an instrument of worship and battle); lute and lyre, stringed instruments used in both popular and sacred music to celebrate; timbrel and dance (suggesting women who danced in the atmosphere of a party, twisting and whirling, suggestive even of labor and childbirth); strings and pipe, a reedy sensuous instrument connected with lustiness; cymbals that tingle, quiver, whir, buzz, and make a crashing sound, all accompanied by a shout of joy, of triumph, even applause.

Finally, who is to praise God? Everything that has breath; everything that breathes the same air as God. This psalm, this call to praise, is in the end utterly universal.

Sermon Starter: Go Crazy

Hear the intensity, the frenzy, the fervor of the praise of God? The words "praise," *hallelu*, repeat again and again. This *hallelu* connects linguistically to a word for madness, craziness. The means of praise—dance and music and shouting—are all borrowed from the secular, sensual realm, as are the instruments named. So a possible sermon in a one-line summary: *If we let go of our staid, reserved worship of God, we may be able to worship God with utter abandon.*

Take the theme of utter abandonment in worship; encourage a more joyful, exuberant expression in worship. Describe the psalmist's secular, sensual means of praise (not just graceful liturgical dance, but twirling and twisting and shouting). This psalm could give permission to explore a variety of musical styles. Focus on the real fervor and imagination buried in some of our traditional modes of praise. Explore the contrast between the way we worship God and the way our culture worships athletes and celebrities. Express the irony of sports fanaticism—so much more visible and wholehearted than our fanaticism about God.

Describe a brass band, including the percussion section that sets the beat, and the cymbalist who crashes at just the right moment. Even the bright cymbal part in a Sousa march or the cool brushing of a jazz cymbalist seem reserved compared to the crashing and clashing of the psalm.

Describe the frenzy and fervor evident when we become sports fans. We abandon all our reserve. We make fools of ourselves, wearing cheeseheads, painting faces and bodies, sporting colors and buttons and logos. We literally go crazy.

How do we restrain ourselves from worshiping God with all we are and have? Why do we limit ourselves to one or two instruments in worship? Why insist on the old favorite hymns and on reverent choral music? How can we behave so sanely when we hear the good news of God's great love for us?

Many of us tend to favor classical space and music. Yet even traditional art, architecture, and music of the church are lavish displays of praise, reflecting the creativity of a great and imaginative God. Soaring cathedrals and cozy brick churches, a Mozart mass and a Bach cantata, stained-glass windows and wood carved pulpits all express human joy and delight in God.

Consider Bach's B minor Mass. As the choir sings of Christ's incarnation and crucifixion, the music moves from haunting melody to a low, groaning dissonance and finally to the silence of death and burial. After a moment the trumpets blast and the choir sings *"et resurrexit,"* Christ is risen!

Yet most audiences sit before that music still and stony-faced. If they feel it, understand it, *believe* it, their faces and their bodies don't show it. We have learned to "control" our emotions. How can we sit still and remain seemingly unaffected by the good news of God that we hear proclaimed week in and week out?

Close with an illustration of a time when mainline church-goers abandoned their stony faces and expressed mind-tingling, body-moving PRAISE! Or find a fitting musical expression and encourage the congregation to respond with fervor.

SERMON STARTER: MIRROR, MIRROR

Explore the reflective imagery of this psalm. The repetition of the word *hallelu*, the intense parallelism of the poetry, the utter inclusivity of the psalm as to the where, why, how, and who of praise all suggest a movement both Godward and outward. The image of the mirror provides a key to the praise of God and its reflection in our lives and in the world. A possible summary: *Created in the image of the Creator, we are made to reflect God's glory to God, self, and the whole of creation.*

Worship is not a one-way movement. It does not begin with our adoration of God. Our worship of God is a reflection of God's very being. It begins with the creative energy of God, which moves outward toward creation. We reflect divine imagination and creativity. In faith we identify ourselves with this glorious God. In right relation with this God, we enjoy God's very being. This is the center of our praise and worship of God.

The Westminster divines asked first about the "chief end" of human existence and answered boldly: "to glorify...to enjoy God forever." Glory and joy go hand in hand; both are contagious. Our praise reflects God's glory, not only back toward God in exuberant worship, but also outward toward the world. To glorify God is to boast, to take pride in God, to make God look good, to associate ourselves with God, to proclaim God's goodness, and to live in a way that reflects well on God.

The glorification of God in worship is not vain or ego-centered. Not the witch in Snow White, who asked in the mirror, "Who's the fairest of them all?" Not Narcissus, who fell in love with his own reflection. God is no narcissist. Rather, God's creative love moves outward.

Our exuberant worship must engender in us love of God and neighbor or it becomes ineffective. Our worship of God mirrors God's great and lavish love toward us; our worship moves us to mirror that love to the world. Our worship is never perfect or complete, yet it calls forth in us our best and most creative energy.

Close this sermon by asking the congregation what kind of mirror it is. As a corporate body, how are we reflecting the joy and glory of God to our world, ourselves, and back to God? Highlight one or two ways in which that "mirroring" gives light to your life.

OFFERING MEDITATION

> The psalmist speaks in superlatives
>> of God's great greatness, God's mighty might.
> The psalmist calls us to exuberant, extravagant praise
>> for we are utterly dependent on
>> this great and extravagant God.
> The psalmist invites us to worship this God
>> by offering God all that we are and have.

It is right to worship this God
  with grateful generosity,
  right to serve God
    with the very currency of our lives,
  right to reflect our love back to God
    with our worldly resources.

OFFERING PRAYER

Gracious, gift-giving God,
  lavish in love and kindness:
You have so freely given us all good things,
  even the inexpressible gift of your son, Jesus.
Receive these gifts for the sake of Christ
  and for the world you love.
May they become a pledge of our love and gratitude
  and of our desire to serve and worship you
  with our very lives.
Amen.

COMMUNION MEDITATION

All good scouts know to "be prepared" for any possible situation. Every good scout who hikes in the woods takes along a survival kit—a jackknife and a flashlight, perhaps chocolate or sugar cubes wrapped in foil, waterproof matches, a small mirror.

Why a mirror? The mirror can catch the light of the sun and reflect it back up and out, so if we get lost we might more easily be found. Someone looking for us, in a plane or on foot, might see the reflected sunlight from that small mirror and find us.

This sacrament is like that mirror. Nowhere do we see so clearly the heart of our faith as in this bread and in this cup. Nowhere does the greatness of God shine as brightly as in the simplicity of this sacrament. Nothing reflects God's glory—the light that seeks us out, finds us, and saves us—as radiantly as these earthly elements. In these simple elements we see the intense light of God's great love for us. God's love shines in our darkness, reflects in our very souls.

So communion is for us a means of survival; of knowing we are lost, yet found; of finding our lives only to lose them again in thankful praise, in grateful gratitude, in loving living.

Come all who are lost, restless, and wandering, for here you will be found.

PRAYER AFTER COMMUNION

> Gracious, gift-giving God,
> > great in glory, lavish in love:
> In this holy meal we have found you.
> In this meal we have been found in you.
> May we, being found and fed,
> > lose ourselves in your love for the world. Amen.

BENEDICTION

> Let the worship of God now begin!
> Go from here with fervor and abandon,
> > prepared to reflect God's great glory
> > and lavish love wherever you go.
> **And may the Triune God be with you:**
> The gracious grace of Christ;
> The fanatic fervor of the Spirit,
> The mighty muchness of God.
> Amen.

Isaiah 11:6–9

Linda McKiernan-Allen

CALL TO WORSHIP

Gather in, one and all!
Expectantly, we come.
Here we lift up God, who offers hope to a hurting
world.
Here we praise God, who creates peace
in a world of pain.
Here God opens our eyes to a vision of shalom.
Let us worship God!

OPENING PRAYER (UNISON)

God, we your creatures stand before you,
eager to see and believe good news!
In this season, we wait.
We worship in anticipation of a Lamb promised
but not yet born.
We come eager to know more of your realm
and yearning to see its fullness.
Stand with us in this hour,
and move us to tiptoe
in readiness for what is to come.
Through your Promised One, Jesus, we pray. Amen.

PRAYER OF CONFESSION

Holy God, every time we hear your vision for the world,
we tremble.

We claim to follow the Prince of Peace, but we hurt and destroy the earth, our neighbors, and ourselves.

We declare our innocence as disciples of the One without sin but continue to buy goods created in oppressive sweatshops.

We claim a preference for widows, children, and the poor, as Jesus did in Galilean ministry, but we participate in economics of preference for those already wealthy.

Forgive us. Remove the shields of selfishness from our eyes and hearts, so we might recognize our place within your realm of love. Restore us to wholeness within your creation. Renew our joy, and mark us with your claim, "They will not hurt or destroy on all my holy mountain." In trust, we pray. Amen.

Words of Assurance

Friends, we serve a God who can create a place where wolves and lambs live together, and a little child shall lead a parade of wild beasts. This God can create a new heaven and a new earth. This God can forgive all our sin and restore all our brokenness. In Jesus, the Christ, God acts in love to make all things new. Thanks be to God!

Prayers of the People

God of Vision, the words of scripture sing in our hearts this season as we prepare to celebrate the birth of Jesus; leopards and goats, lions and calves, and no more destruction on all your holy mountain.

Thank you for the hope, which sparkles like 10,000 twinkling lights, that good can overcome evil, and that true peace will blanket the earth. We're grateful today because your vision of a world restored catches our imagination, and your presence within the world inspires our trust.

We come before you today, conscious that the North American world is caught in a great commercial extravaganza, fueled by the knowledge of what will sell and who will pay. We recognize all around us the frustrations, anger, hurt, and dismay of those who do not know any other way.

We know not only the push toward extravagance, but also the disparity of much of North American life against that of most of the earth. As we sing hymns of "peace on earth," we groan with scenes from natural disasters and recoil from the horror of ethnic battles. We turn away from the knowledge of landmines planted and nuclear weapons tested. We close our eyes to children dumped in trash barrels and families living on trash heaps.

In this sanctuary time, this "safe" time, this separated-from-the-world time, fill us with the knowledge of the Lord. Incorporate us into your vision for the world and make us clear about our place. Then send us back to the world, eager to paint the vision of peace in the lives of those with whom we come in contact.

We pray for our world, our neighbors, and ourselves, through Jesus, the Christ, who embodied your shalom. Amen.

CHILDREN'S SERMON: A PEACEFUL REALM
(BY PATRICIA HATFIELD)

Preparation: Obtain a copy of the painting The Peaceable Realm. *Try your library's print collection or look in a book of early American art. Also, it can be found in the curriculum* Glimpses of the Gospel through Art, *by Devere Ramsay (available from the National Teacher Education Program, 2504 N. Roxboro St., Durham, NC 27704; 919-477-3505; $15.95). You can obtain a small black and white copy for six cents or a color copy for twelve cents of the print contained in* Glimpses *from The University Prints, 21 E. St., Winchester, MA 01890.*

I'd like to share with you this morning a picture painted by Edward Hicks, who lived when America was a new country. Edward Hicks was both a painter and a minister who did not like how some people treated Native Americans (the Indians). Land had been stolen from many tribes. Some people killed Native Americans or made them slaves. Edward Hicks had a dream that America would be a country of peace just like the prophet Isaiah's vision of peace. Here is what the prophet Isaiah said. (*Read the text from your Bible.*)

And here is the picture that Edward Hicks painted. It's called *The Peaceable Realm.* On the right side, Mr. Hicks painted mostly animals. What are some of the animals you see? Which animal has the fiercest looking eyes? What are the animals doing? Many of these animals would normally be afraid of each other. Do you know which animals would be afraid of each other? (*Cow and lion, bear and cow, sheep and goat and the wolf, and the leopard and the children might also be mentioned.*)

How many children do you see in the picture? What are they doing? How would *you* like to play with the animals in the picture? (*Affirm all of the children's responses.*)

Look now to the left side of the picture. More than peace among the animals, Mr. Hicks wanted peace among people. Look at the people on the left. How are they dressed? (*Some wear "suits," and others wear almost nothing at all; some wear hats on their heads, and others wear feathers in their hair.*) Who do you think they are? (*Early American settlers and Indians or Native Americans.*) What do you think they are doing? (*Talking, shaking hands, giving presents.*) The men dressed in suits are Christians called Quakers. They are making an agreement to live with the Indians in peace. We know they really kept their promise! If you were going to paint a picture today of people you'd like to have live in peace, who would you include? (*People of different races, of different gangs; people of different countries; perhaps brothers and sisters in a family or mommies and daddies will be mentioned.*) Even today, we still need the prophet Isaiah's dream of peace, and people to paint and pray to fulfill the dream. Let's pray.

[*Prayer:*] Dear God, thank you for people like the prophet Isaiah and Edward Hicks, who remind us that we can all live together in peace. Help each of us to do our part to make our world a more peaceful place. Amen.

SERMON STARTER: FULL OF KNOWLEDGE

Marilyn vos Savant writes a weekly column in *Parade* magazine in which she answers difficult questions (often math related). She is recognized as the world's most intelligent person and obviously enjoys being challenged by a multitude of questions.

Heloise also writes a regular column that is carried in newspapers. She provides answers to challenging questions that are most often related to home maintenance (kitchen, bathroom, and laundry tips).

Every year at about this time, students begin to cram for final exams. In many colleges and universities these exams provide opportunities for students to write what they know about a multitude of topics. The exams usually come at the completion of a semester of classroom and library work and are presented (and graded) by professors who have taught the class from the knowledge they have.

Occasionally, we come into contact with someone who carries such a wealth of knowledge across so many disciplines and arenas that we acknowledge that person as a "Renaissance" man or woman. That's the Trivial Pursuit partner to grab!

So is that the kind of knowledge that the whole earth will have when God's peaceful realm emerges, the "knowledge of the Lord" from our Isaiah passage this morning? If we all spent the next twenty years in full-time seminary, would we have that kind of knowledge? What about folks who don't learn well from books?

Good news! The "knowledge of the Lord" has very little to do with native intelligence, or family history and connections, or being an A student. It does not serve as the repository for trivial information that could advance you to Trivial Pursuit finals. Rather, it is Isaiah's way of saying something about a right relationship of humans to God. We might be more likely to say "the earth will have faith," or "the earth will believe" than to use the psalmist's language, "the earth will be full of the knowledge of the Lord."

And what is this right relationship? Isaiah gives us a picture as a metaphor with the multitude of animals and children in Isaiah 11:6–8. Edward Hicks used the text to make a political/ethical/theological statement in his painting *The Peaceable Realm*. (*If the children have seen* The Peaceable Realm *during Children's Sermon, refer to that here. If you have copies in the bulletin or copies handed to each worshiper, take some time to tell the story of Edward Hicks and use the picture as an image of what a "right relationship" looks like in the painting.*)

The Hebrew poetry of Isaiah 11 points clearly to the effect of "knowledge of the Lord." A time will come when the whole earth is incorporated into God's peaceable realm. If we could draw a word picture of that time, we might say we'll recognize that time has come when (*with a smile*):

- carnivores and vegetarians can sit at the table together
- labor and management fairly arbitrate between themselves
- domestic violence exists only in memory, and shelters are turned into museums
- adults speak honestly about their fears of other races, rather than promoting racial hatred
- children in Africa no longer die from dehydration and diarrhea
- children in Asia no longer are "dumped" because they're the wrong gender
- children all over the world have sufficient food, clean water, and decent housing
- gun violence in the United States is only history

We'll recognize the peaceable realm because "they will not hurt or destroy on all my holy mountain, for the earth will be full of the knowledge of the Lord as the waters cover the sea."

Sermon Starter: The Energizer Gift

December is the time in North American life that many people spend looking for "that perfect gift." Even folks who are not Christian get involved in parties, gift exchanges, and festive times. Lists are made, shopping expeditions planned, and much advertising focuses on gifts that will "keep on giving."

And we use some of the same language in the church when we speak of God's great gift (meaning Jesus). The prophet Isaiah, however, pictures God's great gift differently than the writers of Matthew and Luke. For Isaiah, there is a shoot from the stump of Jesse (Bible language for a descendant in Jesse's family line), whose reign will be marked by peace and harmony.

It's clear we're not there.

Look as far away as the natural disasters around the world; look as close as the domestic violence in our neighbor's home (or in our own home).

Look at generations of people scarred by war in the Congo or by dependence on a disappearing welfare system in America.

Look at systemic oppression of migrant workers and impossible expectations of fast-track careers by parents of young children.

It's anything but "the peaceable realm" in the world we know.

Nor can we find God's deepest peace in many of our own lives when we walk the "don't ask—don't tell" tightrope, when our "affluenza" threatens to bankrupt us, when we can't remember the last day we told the truth to others and to ourselves. It's certainly not "the peaceable realm" either in corporate or individual life.

So what does God intend? Isaiah pictures animals and children operating with one another in peace and safety. Then Isaiah boldly declares: "They will not hurt or destroy on all my holy mountain." It may not be complete or even stating the picture in the positive. But it's basic. No more hurting. No more destruction. Let's start with at least that.

If this is God's intention, what needs to happen to move the world in that direction?

Do you remember the book from some years past *All I Ever Needed to Know I Learned in Kindergarten*? Here's another place where that may be true. The world could become more a place of God's basic intention if we realized we're not on the planet just by ourselves or for ourselves. When we move out of the adolescent stance of "meet my needs; to hell with yours," we can remember to share, to take turns, to hold hands with one another, and to say thank you to the One who helps us.

In this season of the year, when we search for the perfect gift (the one that will keep on giving…that Energizer gift), here it is, right in front of us! It's a commitment to not hurt or destroy in God's whole creation.

(If you have a particular program, ministry, or mission that fits this category, build from this point on the specifics of what you want the congregation to do.)

Our world is not a peaceable realm today. But in this season of gifts, we can help each other step toward the peaceable realm by our action. In Jewish understanding, it's a mitzvah, a good deed done for another. In Christian understanding, it's "doing unto others as you would have them do to you." Like many of the best gifts, it's one that gives to both the recipient and the giver.

And in the end, our own efforts put us more clearly within the picture of God's peaceable realm, where we are full of the knowledge of the Lord.

OFFERING MEDITATION

What a Hollywood disaster this would be! Wolves, lambs, leopards, goats, cows, lions, and fatlings (what is a fatling, anyway?) all peacefully going on parade behind a little child. No high-speed race cars, no exploding high rises, no double-crossing, shifty-eyed detectives.

So what makes us believe this is a vision worth our while? Why is a "peaceable realm" something we might support with our time, our money, and our energy? Not because it's sexy or jazzy or Hollywood exciting.

But because it holds the promise of the wholeness God intends for creation. And when we line up behind the One who brought everything out of nothing, we eagerly anticipate what that One can bring out of our lives. Today we come to put our finances where we want our hearts to be, along with all the lions, leopards, and lambs we can find.

OFFERING PRAYER

Out of your extravagant abundance, you continue to shower us with blessings, Loving God. Thank you for all good gifts and for this opportunity to put our money and our hearts to work for your peaceable realm. Accept what we bring, inspire us to generous giving, and encourage us to join the parade. We pray through Christ, who goes before us. Amen.

COMMUNION MEDITATION

For many of us, the table around which we gathered as children to eat our meals holds a special place in our hearts. There we were nourished by those who loved us and by the food that had been prepared. There we came in childish joy, in adolescent rebellion, in occasional returns as a young adult. There the rhythm of life found a beat.

Although we may not have a family gathering around the table on a daily basis, we do find something of that spirit as we gather around the communion table on a regular basis. Imagine what God's perspective might be as we come to this table. God, who envisioned that "the wolf shall live with the lamb, the leopard shall lie down with the kid" surely finds something of that same challenge with us. (*Use a gentle hand in describing the differences within the congregation gathered, but enough clarity for the truth to shine.*) Here the self-satisfied kneels next to the anguished, the mother of ten stands beside the longing mid-life single. Here we find Gucci shoes and used Keds. Here the gurgles of an infant swirl into memories of an octogenarian.

Here we find broken bread, which somehow binds us together into one body. Here the cup poured out brings this varied rainbow of humanity into one vessel.

Here, as the babe of Bethlehem becomes both the man of sorrows and the triumphant Lamb of God, we catch a glimpse of God so encompassing, it's like the waters that cover the sea. Come to the table, for all is ready!

BENEDICTION

Children of God, arise!
Go from this place nourished by bread and cup,
inspired by a vision of God's peace,
eager to live "as if" the whole world were God's holy mountain,
where no one will ever again hurt or destroy.

Matthew 1:18–25

Diana Hagewood Smith

The Matthew text introduces us to Jesus as the child born in the lineage of David and claimed as a child of the Holy Spirit. This text holds a central position in scripture's affirmation of Jesus as "God with us."

A CALL TO WORSHIP (BASED ON PSALM 85 AND MATTHEW 1)

We come to worship God.
Who can stand in God's presence?
We *can* stand, for God is with us, not to punish,
    but to save.
Restore us, Lord God,
    and bring your new reality to birth in us:
Surprise us, Lord, even as you surprised Joseph,
    as we worship you this day.

OPENING PRAYER

Fiercely loving God,
    you love us like a father and
    protect us like a mother.
Be with us as we turn to you.
Lift the burdens to which we cling.
Give us instead the burden of Christ:
    compassion for others and gentle refuge,
    that we may grow into your image.
In the name of Christ. Amen.

PRAYER OF CONFESSION

Gracious and graceful God, you come to us in surprising ways, and we are dismayed. You offer us new beginnings, but we cling to the past. You invite us to go boldly into the future; we timidly wish for the comfortable and familiar. You offer us new companions in our journey; we long for the safe and predictable folks we know. Forgive us. Forgive us, and save us from our sins. Amen.

WORDS OF ASSURANCE (BASED ON ISAIAH 49:15; 66:13)

Our God says, "Can a woman forget her nursing child or show no compassion for the child of her womb? Even these may forget, yet I will not forget you; as a mother comforts her child, so I will comfort you." Sisters and brothers, take comfort; in Christ's name, we are forgiven!

PRAYERS OF THE PEOPLE

After "Lord, in your mercy," the people respond, **"Hear our prayer."**

Together, let us pray for the people of this congregation: [*Silence*]

Gracious God, as you brought Joseph to you, so draw us together to worship you in spirit and in truth. Wherever there is division or unease, give us your loving Spirit that does not ignore difficulties, but loves beyond. *Lord, in your mercy.*

Let us pray for the church: [*Silence*]

God of many names, as you spoke in dreams and visions, so you continue to share with your world. Help us reach out to brothers and sisters across lines of culture, class, language, and creed. Remind us we are known as your church not by right doctrine, but by right loving. *Lord, in your mercy.*

Let us pray for those who are suffering: [*Silence*]

Merciful God, as the story of a pregnant, unwed teen inspires our care, so you care for all who are suffering from wounds of body, mind, or spirit. Lift the burdens of those who struggle with depression or despair. To those bowed down by sin, speak your comforting word of unconditional love. Teach us to love others with your forgiving love and to speak words that heal instead of hurt. *Lord, in your mercy.*

Let us pray for those terrorized by war and violence, far away and in our own backyards: [*Silence*]

Righteous God, bring speedy relief and justice to all who suffer from oppression and violence. Grant solace to those violated by hate-filled words and destructive relationships. Restore those damaged by backroom whispers. *Lord, in your mercy.*

Let us pray for our enemies: [*Silence*]

Forgiving God, teach us, as you taught Joseph, to let go of hatred and curb our desire for revenge. Help us to see the face of Christ even in those who have hurt us. *Lord, in your mercy.*

Let us pray for those held in our thoughts this day: [*Silence, or congregation may speak names aloud*] Lord, you know each of our needs. We entrust them to you. *Lord, in your mercy.*

In Jesus' name—God with us—Emmanuel. Amen.

CHILDREN'S SERMON: JOSEPH AND MARY
(BY PATRICIA HATFIELD)

This morning I want to talk to you about fathers. One special father in the Bible is Joseph. Do you know who Joseph was the father of? Yes, Joseph was the father of Jesus! But did you know that Joseph wasn't too sure about being the father of Jesus at first?

Joseph loved Mary so much he asked her to marry him. Mary said yes! They became engaged. But before the wedding, Joseph found out Mary was pregnant. This was a big problem because you were not supposed to be pregnant before you married. Joseph was very upset. According to the law, he could end his engagement to Mary. Then, however, people would know that Mary was pregnant. They might believe she was a sinner and treat her badly. Joseph did not want this to happen to Mary. So he decided to end the engagement without saying anything out loud about it.

Just when Joseph decided to do that, an angel of the Lord appeared to Joseph in a dream! The angel said, "Joseph, don't be afraid to take Mary as your wife. The baby that she is carrying is from the Holy Spirit. She will give birth to a son, and you are to name him Jesus."

When Joseph awoke, he immediately took Mary as his wife. When she had given birth to a son, Joseph adopted the child, named the baby Jesus, and raised him as his very own.

After Jesus was born, we don't hear very much about Joseph. But just from this one story we know that Joseph was a very kind and loving man. He had a difficult decision to make and he trusted God to help him make the right choice. Because Joseph did trust God, Jesus was raised in a good and loving family until the time came for him to tell the people the good news: Jesus is the Son of God! Let's pray.

[*Prayer:*] Dear God, thank you for fathers. Please help all fathers trust in you when they have difficult decisions to make. God, please help us talk to you when we have difficult decisions too. Amen.

Sermon Starter: Background

Most scholars believe the gospel of Matthew was written to a predominantly Jewish congregation, probably located in Antioch, that had only recently broken with or been forced out of the local synagogue. The gospel seems to answer the twofold question, "What do we do with our Jewish heritage now that we are no longer a part of the larger Jewish community?" and "How do we understand the increasingly Gentile nature of the church?"

Matthew addresses the first question, that of the church's relationship to Judaism, by emphasizing Jesus as one who fulfilled the Jewish scriptures in a completely unexpected manner. The genealogy of Jesus found in Matthew 1:1–17 takes the form of three sets of fourteen generations. This genealogy explains how Jesus, the son of Mary, can also be called the son of David through his father, Joseph. Matthew 1:18–25 tells us how Jesus can be the Son of David, when his lineage is traced through Joseph, who is not his biological father. In verse 23 the quotation from Isaiah 7:14 is not exact (in the Isaiah passage, the mother of the child names him): "*They* [italics mine] shall name him Emmanuel." In verse 25, Joseph names him, acknowledging the child as a member of the family of David.

SERMON STARTER: RISKY FATHERHOOD

Two sisters were examining a picture of Mary and the infant Jesus. The younger sister said, "But where's Joseph?" Her older sister thought a moment, then replied, "Joseph is taking the picture."

Joseph is often the missing person in the Christmas picture. We know who Joseph is. We have to find someone to play Joseph in every Christmas pageant, someone to lead the donkey to Bethlehem and confront the innkeeper. We don't think of Joseph as a real, flesh-and-blood hero of the faith.

Joseph is only mentioned in a few passages dealing with Jesus' birth and in Luke's account of the time that Jesus frightened his parents when he remained behind in Jerusalem to teach in the temple. We don't know how or when Joseph died.

Matthew spends a great deal of time telling us about the genealogy of Jesus. This may be puzzling to us, but it was important to the original readers of Matthew's gospel (Matthew's first readers were probably Jewish Christians who would have only lately left the synagogue), who wanted to understand how their Christian faith related to their Jewish heritage and to the Jewish scriptures. Further, they were concerned about the growing Gentile nature of the church and their relationship to Gentile Christianity. Matthew carefully assured them that Jesus didn't cancel out the heritage of the Jews or the obligations of righteous behavior, but fulfilled them in surprising new ways. Matthew tells the story of Jesus' birth through the perspective of Joseph, a righteous man.

Matthew tells us Joseph and Mary were betrothed. In ancient Israel, a betrothal was more than just an engagement; it was the first step in a marriage and served as a legally binding contract. It was typical for the bride to remain in her parents' home following the betrothal, for a period of probably a year. At the end of the betrothal period the bridegroom would bring her to his own house. During this time, she was legally considered his wife. Mary became pregnant, and

Joseph found out. Everyone else might have suspected Joseph and Mary had simply jumped the gun (not the ideal family model!).

An older pastor once declared, "Don't ever mess with Father's Day." Sometimes it's tempting to preach the traditional Father-on-the-pedestal-greeting-card Father's Day sermon. However, for many people, Mother's Day and Father's Day are painful. For those who struggle with infertility and those whose mothers or fathers were neglectful or abusive, these holidays are dreaded reminders of wounds that never fully heal. When we acknowledge these concerns honestly, a number of listeners may feel free to express their deep discomfort with celebrations of family. This may allow a sense of relief at finally allowing their experiences to be recognized as a part of the church's experience.

Read the story of Joseph through the lens of those who are stepparents and parents by adoption. "Family" sometimes means "blood relatives," but sometimes love, respect, and shared values bring families together. All families reflect, in some degree, our relationship as children of God. The risky fatherhood of Joseph may help model an expanded understanding of the way God creates families.

God created a family with Jesus, Joseph, and Mary, from which we all can learn of God's love, recognizing there is NO "perfect" family...no, not one!

Offering Meditation

Joseph dreamed of "God with us"and came to know his son, Jesus, who did not cling to the riches of his divinity, but opened his hands and his heart to be God's generous gift for the world. We experience this as compassion for the physical and spiritual needs of all God's children. Today you are invited to live as "God with us," by giving generously in response to a world in need (*appeal by naming specific needs*).

Offering Prayer

Ever-loving God, we thank you for these gifts. Bless those who give generously and those who receive graciously, that they and we might be your instruments of justice, righteousness, and peace. Amen.

COMMUNION MEDITATION

Five women are mentioned in the genealogy of Matthew 1: Tamar, Rahab, Ruth, "the wife of Uriah," and Mary. All of these women stand out in some way as unique, daring, and significant. In fact, their behavior was often shocking. These were not plaster saints, but women with guts and tenacity. In a culture and situations where they were ostensibly powerless, all of them risked public contempt or physical danger to win and to protect their children or other family members.

Joseph also risks much to accept the angel's assurance that Mary is pregnant by the action of the Holy Spirit and will give birth to the Savior. The risks do not end when he takes Mary into his house. Obeying the will of God means taking a pregnant woman to Bethlehem, fleeing from Herod's soldiers into Egypt, and eventually, relocating to Nazareth.

God risked much in the Incarnation, and God continues to risk much by entrusting ministry to us. God uses very human people in very human situations and nourishes us with something as simple as bread and wine. In this meal we are fortified and enabled to risk much in ministry, just as Tamar and Ruth, Rahab and Mary, the wife of Uriah, and Joseph risked much to be faithful to God's command. Those who accept the risks of God's invitation are nourished at this table. Come, eat, drink, and be satisfied.

BENEDICTION

Go as risk-takers,
    for God has nourished you with bread and cup.
Go as new creatures,
    for God is saving you from your sin.
Go as children of God,
    for God will be with us all. Amen.

Mark 1:1–15

Susanne VanderLugt

PREPARING FOR THE SERVICE

The most helpful resources for preparation would be Ched Myers' interpretations of Mark in *Binding the Strong Man: A Political Reading of Mark's Story of Jesus* (Maryknoll, N.Y.: Orbis Books, 1988), and *Who Will Roll Away This Stone? Discipleship Queries for First World Christians* (Maryknoll, N.Y.: Orbis Books, 1994).

CALL TO WORSHIP

> The purple dawn gives way to glorious day,
> > and the landscape is transformed before our very eyes.
> So too God enters our lives,
> > touches the deep recesses of our hearts,
> > and we are changed.
> Let us worship God.

OPENING PRAYER

> God, blessed be your holy name
> > for you are steadfast in love
> > and unwavering in faithfulness.
> In the waters of baptism
> > you have claimed us as your own
> > and made us partners in the mending
> > of all creation.

Bring us now into your presence
>   and fill us with such longing for your realm
>   that we may turn our worship into witness
>   and follow where you lead.
Through Jesus Christ,
>   to whom with you and the Spirit, one holy God,
>   be honor and praise, now and forever. Amen.

PRAYER OF CONFESSION

Holy and Gracious God, you sent Jesus,
>   your Beloved Child,
>   to reconcile us to you and to each other.
Yet time and time again we turn away from you.
We come knowing our need for repentance
>   and seeking your forgiveness.
When we refuse to look
at the brokenness of our own lives
>   and the hurt we may have caused others,
>   when we do not heed your call
>   to justice
>   and compassion,
>   when we fail to trust in the power of your love
>   and let fear overcome us,
>   forgive us, we pray.
Renew us with remembrance of baptism
>   by your Holy Spirit,
>   that we may live as your people. Amen.

WORDS OF ASSURANCE

Even when our past mistakes condemn us,
>   God is stronger than our guilt.
Even when temptations lead us astray,
>   God's will is stronger than our will.
God's love revealed in Jesus Christ
>   is the sure sign of this promise.
We are a new people—ransomed, healed, restored,
>   forgiven.
Thanks be to God!

PRAYERS OF THE PEOPLE

Generous and Loving God, we give thanks and praise
for the wisdom of your Word
and the hope of your promises.
We thank you for your never-failing grace
that shapes and reshapes us
and sends us out to speak your word of life.
Above all we give thanks for the gift of Jesus Christ,
for illuminating the world
through his baptism, teaching, and resurrection.
Merciful and compassionate God,
we lift to you our concern
for our brothers and sisters who are suffering:
for refugees;
for victims of racism;
for those who are challenged
physically and mentally;
for children who suffer the pain of abuse;
for those who have more than they need,
yet feel empty;
for those whose self-esteem is eroded
by unemployment.
Give us the will to embody your healing love
that we may walk with those who mourn,
who doubt, who fear.
Give us eyes of faith to see the old world
changing into a new world
where peace and justice reign
and the cries of all are heard.
Give us courage to proclaim the way things could be
in the midst of what they are.
And now, O God, wrap your grace
around our innermost needs
as we place before you the prayers of our hearts.
We gather these and all our prayers,
turning to you
as our Mother who watches over us,
as **Our Father, who art in heaven...**

CHILDREN'S SERMON: THE DOVE (BY PATRICIA HATFIELD)

Preparation: Bring a real dove if you can obtain one (contact a local birding or homing pigeon club) or a pretend or toy dove or picture of a dove.

This morning I brought a special friend to visit with us. (*Show the dove.*) Does anyone know who this creature of God is? This is a bird called a dove. Doves are a special bird in the Bible. Do any of you know a Bible story with a dove in it? (*The creation story, Noah's Ark*).

One story with a dove in it is the story of Noah. Remember? (*Yes!*) Noah built a big ark and gathered all the animals, two by two, onto the ark. For forty days it rained and rained, and all the earth was flooded. But God remembered Noah and all the animals and made a wind blow to dry up the rain. Noah wanted to be sure it was safe to let the animals out of the ark, so he sent out a dove. The dove found no place to set its feet, and it returned to the ark. Noah waited seven days and sent out the dove again. The dove came back to Noah in the evening. There in its beak was a freshly plucked olive leaf, so Noah knew the water was going away. Noah waited seven more days and again sent out the dove. This time it did not return, so Noah let the animals out of the ark.

Another story with a dove is a story of Mary and Joseph. Eight days after Jesus was born, his parents took their newborn baby to the temple in Jerusalem. The parents offered two doves as a "thanks offering" to God. Simeon, an old man who loved God, had received a message from God saying he would see God's son before he died. The day Simeon saw Joseph and Mary dedicate their baby to God and give God the gift of two doves, Simeon knew—this was the Son of God! Simeon took the baby Jesus in his arms. He praised and thanked God that the Lord had allowed him to live so very long and see the Son of God.

And in today's story, Jesus is baptized in the Jordan River. As he came out of the water, the Spirit of God came upon Jesus like a dove and the voice of God said, "This is my Son, whom I love very much." (*Use your empty hands or the toy dove to lower the dove over the head of a child to illustrate the story.*)

Doves are part of several important stories in the Bible. Whenever you read a Bible story with a dove in it, be on the lookout for God's power at work! Can you see any doves in our sanctuary? (*Point out any doves in the stained glass or elsewhere in the sanctuary.*) Let's pray.

[*Prayer:*] Dear God, thank you for sending beautiful doves. Whenever we see a dove or read about a dove, help us to be like Simeon, praising you for your Son, Jesus. Amen.

SERMON STARTER: POWERLESS

One day I was backing out of my driveway. There was a fellow walking by, so I waited for him to pass. When I turned to check for oncoming traffic, I caught sight of the back of his shirt. With individual iron-on letters on the back of his shirt he had written the word, POWERLESS.

Can you see that fellow's shirt? At times, some folks at church wear it. Sometimes any of us might wear it, those times when the life-destroying forces of evil seem to be too much in control.

Not everyone wears a shirt with that word on it. Into the very center of this gospel story Mark brings a young man from a northern town in Galilee. Jesus of Nazareth walks out into the Jordan River and is baptized by John. When Jesus comes up out of the water, the skies open and the Spirit descends upon him like a dove. And a voice comes from heaven: "You are my Son, the Beloved; with you I am well pleased."

The word on his shirt may well have been "The Stronger One." The one whom John proclaimed "more powerful than I" has come. In the wilderness Satan banks on rendering Jesus powerless. But Jesus emerges from his wilderness struggles as the victor, ready to begin his ministry. This Stronger One changes the order of things and brings people into a whole new way of being and living. In language unfamiliar to many of us, we could say Jesus offers us *apocalyptic* hope.

What does apocalyptic hope look like?

(*Lift up other Marcan stories filled with the promise that God is transforming the world: the man with the unclean spirit* [1:21–27], *stilling the storm* [4:35–41], *healing the Gerasene demoniac* [5:1–20], *the healing of Bartimaeus* [10:46–52].)

It looks like Bartimaeus sprang up onto his feet, threw off his cloak, and ran into the power of God's life-changing love. Jesus tells Bartimaeus, now healed of his blindness, to go on his way. But Bartimaeus does not go his own way. He chooses to begin a new journey and follow Jesus' way, not knowing where it will take him.

What does living in apocalyptic hope look like for us?

It looks like the former mayor of Toronto with a hundred homeless persons gathered around him at the corner of Dundas and Sherbourne. A media person shoves a television camera in his face, and he responds, "I don't want to live in a city where people die in the streets. I'm willing to share my wealth and energy to make sure it doesn't happen."

Living in apocalyptic hope looks like three soldiers in Hebron, two Israeli and one Palestinian, standing close together, having a conversation, their heads thrown back in laughter.

It looks like us gathered here this morning with the expectation that Christ will meet us, and in the meeting our lives will be different. All around us, it's business as usual. All around us, life-destroying forces wait to take control of us. Yet we gather to worship.

As we break open the Word of God together, Christ is present.

As we share a meal of bread and wine, Christ is present.

In the presence of the Beloved Son of God everything changes. It's a new order. There are no distinctions, no divisions. No one need wear a shirt with the iron-on letters that spell *powerless*.

In the presence of the Beloved Son of God love is stronger than evil, life is more powerful than death.

We can trust this One. Jesus Christ is strong enough to lead us out into the world to counter life-destroying forces, strong enough to inspire us to share our wealth and energy, strong enough to put words on our lips that have the power to redeem. When Jesus Christ, the Stronger One, enters our lives and our community, nothing can ever be the same again.

SERMON STARTER: A FIRST-PERSON NARRATIVE

The banks of the river were lined with people. We curious about the man called John. He was strange and wild looking. Many thought he was Elijah returned. He preached with electrifying power. When he invited folks to come into the water, to die to their old selves and receive new life, several did! They walked right out, clothes and all, to the place John was standing, up to his waist in water.

I wasn't sure. Part of me wanted to go, but I had my tradition. Here was something new. I didn't think it was for me. Still, I could not take my eyes off what was happening out there. I inched my way through the crowd to get a closer look.

I saw a good-looking man in his thirties wading out toward John. I could tell from his dress he was a Galilean. We believed nothing good could ever come from Galilee.

I stood on the edge of the river thinking, "I'm okay the way I am. I've already found favor with God. Maybe John's offer of repentance and the forgiveness of sins does not really apply to me. It's for the poor, like that guy walking out there now.

I watched.

I watched as John took him in his arms and laid him in the water. The northerner went completely under. When he emerged, I saw the skies open and the Spirit descend upon him like the most beautiful, graceful, pure white dove. I heard a voice coming from heaven. I'll never forget the words: "You are my Son, the Beloved; with you I am well pleased."

I looked all around. No one else seemed to see or hear what I had. I looked to the river. The beautiful bird was gone, and the man was walking back to shore. Had I been dreaming?

Then the northerner was standing beside me. I looked into his face. His whole face was absolutely radiant. He held out his hand, and I took it. He helped me step from the shore into the water. I ran out to John, and he baptized me.

My life has never been the same since.

After, I searched the shoreline for God's Beloved. He was gone.

But I'm keeping watch, waiting to see the sign of the Spirit (that beautiful, graceful, pure white bird) and listening for God's voice to announce, "You are my beloved. With you I am well pleased."

(*Step out of the "first person," perhaps by moving from one place to another, pausing, and changing your demeanor and voice.*)

I have seen and heard it a few times. Always when I did not expect it. Always with the most unlikely people.

Like that teenager in confirmation class at church. Halfway through, she discovered she had not been baptized like all the others. To be confirmed she had to be baptized. There was *no way* she was going to stand up in front of the whole congregation, the only one with water being splashed all over her. She was angry with her parents, angry with the minister, angry! You could tell she was wrestling with an important decision. She wanted baptism but she didn't want a spectacle.

I was in the gathered crowd that Confirmation Sunday. When it came time for the young people to be confirmed, she was there in the midst of them. She stepped forward to be splashed with water and marked with the sign of the cross. The minister laid hands on her head and blessed her.

The girl's head came up and she looked out into the crowd. A smile! Her eyes sparkled. Her whole face shone. Then I saw the Spirit descend upon her like a beautiful, graceful, pure white dove, and I heard God's voice, "You are my beloved; with you I am well pleased."

Then there was Joseph. I don't know his name, but that is what I call him. I see him every day on my way to and from work. He walks Yonge Street between Sheppard and Eglinton. In the summer he walks barefoot. He's tall and thin. His hair is matted in dreadlocks. This winter he has a new, bright emerald green wool coat. He puts it over his other clothes and wraps it around himself like a kimono.

We were in the local restaurant having a bite to eat. I saw Joseph put his hand on the restaurant door. The waiter dropped everything and ran. I heard the waiter shout, "No!

You can't come in. We have nothing for you." Joseph looked right into that waiter's face and smiled. All the people in the restaurant heard his parting words: "That's okay, man; you have a good evening now."

The next thing I knew the waiter was out there on the pavement in that bitterly cold January night, shirtsleeves and all. And there it was again—the beautiful, graceful, pure white dove sheltering the two of them with its great broad wings. And I heard God's voice, "You are my beloved; with you I am well pleased."

When the waiter came in from the cold, he was definitely different. You could tell by the way he went about his work, the way he related to his customers, the way he was with his coworkers.

I remembered my own baptism and felt something open up inside.

Can you remember yours? Remember. Breathe deeply into that memory and listen. Can you hear the whisper? "You are my beloved; with you I am well pleased."

OFFERING MEDITATION

Handel's *Messiah* and the musical *Godspell* etch Isaiah's words into our minds and hearts: "Prepare the way of the Lord, make his paths straight."

The question is: "How can we possibly prepare the way of the Lord?"

Currently every major city in this country faces a crisis of homelessness. We live in the wealthiest, lushest part of God's garden. Yet family homelessness and child poverty are on the rise. Surely God will not be pleased until no child goes hungry at night, no person dies out in the cold, and no parents suffer the anguish of homelessness for their family.

Our offerings this morning cannot solve all these problems. Still, they do signal our desire to prepare the way of the Lord. So let us listen for the voice that cries out to us from the wilderness, "Prepare the way of the Lord, make his paths straight." Then let us offer our tithes, our gifts, and our imaginations, that we may respond in lifesaving ways.

PRAYER OF DEDICATION

> Gracious God, weaver of life's design,
>> we place before you the threads of our work,
>> all our seemingly insignificant words and deeds.
> We offer them with a portion
>> of our financial resources,
>> seeking to wait on you
>> as the angels did in the wilderness.
> Use these gifts and our good intentions, we pray,
>> to weave your new creation. Amen.

COMMUNION MEDITATION

Jesus came proclaiming the good news: "The realm of God is at hand!" Today we proclaim the same good news as we prepare to share a feast at the table of our Lord. We gather in hope. We bring the expectation that here Christ will encounter us and we will be changed. Here we find food that sustains and strengthens us for our way. Here there is a place for everyone:

> Those whose hearts are broken,
>> and whose spirits are wounded,
> those who are anxious about tomorrow,
>> and those who hunger
>> to live closer to the heart of God.
>> Come and taste the wholesome bread of new life.
>> Come and sip the sweet wine of salvation.
>> Come, for the time is fulfilled,
>> and God's realm is come near.

BENEDICTION

> Like the air we breathe,
>> the grace of God surrounds us.
> Like the dawn of a new day,
>> the hope of Christ renews us.
> Like the ground we walk on,
>> the sustaining power of the Holy Spirit
>> strengthens us.
> Therefore, go into the world with daring hearts
>> and tell out the good news of God. Amen.

Luke 10:38—11:4

Peggy McClanahan

The Luke text introduces us to Luke's portrayal of Jesus' relationship with women and continues through Jesus' teaching the disciples to pray. The familiar characters of Mary and Martha and the familiar words of the Lord's Prayer help many identify themselves within these encounters with Jesus.

Setting the Scene

Consider "sculpting" this scripture text, with Mary and Martha on one side of the chancel and the disciples on the other. As the text is read, have a "sculptor" move Martha and then the questioning disciple from an "at ease" stance to a physical petitioning form to show their requests of Jesus. Have the "sculptor" use imagination, including extending Martha's hands toward the person reading the text, with a foot placed forward to indicate movement toward the voice of the story. The disciple might have hands together in prayer or be kneeling.

Call to Worship

God's word awaits us.
God's word is among us.
Christ bids us come and listen.
**Like Mary, we are led by eager hearts,
    and like Martha,**

we are distracted by many things.
Let us lay aside what does not matter.
Let us listen to the One who matters most.
Come, Lord Jesus, be our guest.
Make our hearts your home.
Make our time your own.
Make us ready to listen.

Opening Prayer (In Unison or Led by a Worship Leader)

Gather us into your wisdom, Holy Teacher,
   that your word might come alive within us.
Gather us into your word,
   that it might work within us
   to shape our faith and work.
Gather us together,
   that we might be united in our work and worship.
Amen.

Prayer of Confession

Merciful God, we confess our lives are driven by many desires that distract us from you. We sometimes seek to impress, when what we need is simply a listening ear. We sometimes work hard to please, when what we need is simply some time together. We sometimes get so busy doing what's always been done, we simply cannot see a better way.
   Forgive us for rushing into paths that do not lead to you.
   Forgive us for living in ways that do not give life to ourselves and others.
Live within us and live among us, that we might live. Amen.
   (*Invite the congregation to offer their individual prayers of confession in silence.*)

Words of Assurance

Christ's way is true and God's love is sure.
When we put aside what does not matter to God
   and seek God's mercy,
   God forgives our foolish ways and
   leads us in a new way,

full of hope and love.
Thanks be to God!

PRAYERS OF THE PEOPLE

You are the one, Gentle Teacher, who shows us "what we are meant to do and be." You help us know when the things we expect of ourselves and others are not truly important. You gather us into your work and way of living, where we can discover what matters most. We give you thanks that you take time for us and draw us into your own time, where we can keep the difficulties of life in perspective.

We lift unto you the joys and cares and concerns of our lives:

(The congregation may name aloud their joys and concerns, or the liturgist may have them from the congregation in written form. Specific petitions may be spoken after naming each concern. Included may be petitions:)

- for shut-ins or those who are ill who were not named by the congregation
- for significant events in the life of the congregation and its members and friends
- for current events in the world, the nation, or the community
- for specific ministries of the local congregation
- for specific ministries of the wider church (such as missionaries, denominational programs, ecumenical ministries, other congregations)

We lift these prayers unto you, Giver and Shaper of Life, that you might hear our joys and needs and be at work among us. Comfort those in pain or distress; guide those who are confused or in difficulty; sustain those who are weary with the responsibilities of life.

Hear now the prayers we have voiced and those that echo within the silence of our hearts. We ask it in the name of Jesus Christ, our Savior and Guide. Amen.

(The words "what we are meant to do and be" are from the hymn "I Am the Light of the World" by Jim Strathdee, © 1969 by Jim Strathdee, Desert Flower Music, P.O. Box 1476, Carmichael CA 95609.)

CHILDREN'S SERMON: TEACH ME (BY PATRICIA HATFIELD)

Preparation: Have available a bookmark for each student.

One day, as Jesus and his disciples were traveling from place to place teaching and healing the people, they came to a village. There a woman named Martha invited Jesus to come to her house. Martha was a very good cook. She immediately went to the kitchen to prepare a delicious meal for Jesus. But Martha's sister, Mary, did not go to the kitchen. Instead, Mary sat down by Jesus and listened to his teaching.

Martha was so upset over all the work she had to do that she came and said, "Jesus, don't you care that my sister has left me to do all the work by myself? Tell her to come and help me!"

But Jesus said, "Martha, Martha! You worry about so many things. There is just one thing you need to worry about. Mary has chosen the right thing: She has chosen to learn from me about how to love God and how to love other people."

What are some ways we can learn from Jesus, or about Jesus? (*Read the Bible, go to church, go to Sunday school, from parents, being with other Christians.*) Those are all very good ways to learn about Jesus. Grown-ups do many of these things, too. Let's ask them. (*Ask the congregation to respond by raising their hands.*) How many of you read the Bible? Go to Sunday school? Participate in other church activities? (*Name specifics.*)

Learning is very important; Jesus says it's the most important thing. To help you to learn more and more about Jesus, I want to encourage each of you to read (or have your parents read to you) from the Bible every day. To help you, I have a bookmark so you can mark your place, and each night you will remember which Bible story you are to read next. Let's pray.

[*Prayer:*] Dear God, we thank you that we can learn about you from Jesus. We thank you for the Bible, for friends at church, and for Sunday school teachers who love us. Help us learn more and more about you every day. Amen.

SERMON STARTER: THE LIFE OF EACH INDIVIDUAL

Those who are Marthas know immediately how Martha feels as she scurries to keep the glasses filled and the fig tray replenished while roasting the lamb, supervising the sauces, and setting out the cheeses. Her sister Mary sits enraptured at Jesus' feet, either oblivious to or ignoring the multitude of tasks to be done. Whichever, Martha simmers and seethes at Mary's leisure until she can hold it in no more. "Tell my sister to help me," she finally explodes to Jesus.

To Martha's surprise, Jesus offers no apologies for detaining Mary from her tasks. Instead, he chides his good friend Martha for being anxious about so many things and defends Mary for having made a better choice! Poor Martha! She is just trying to be a good hostess, putting out the royal feast for such a royal guest, and he does not even have the grace to excuse her sister to come help.

This is a story about Mary, Martha, and Jesus. Martha receives Jesus into her house. Conversation flows between Mary and Jesus. Mary is described simply as "Martha's sister." Jesus focuses not on Martha's work, but on her anxiety. This story may not be about Martha's wanting help with her work at all! Despite our reading "into" the text, Martha didn't ask Mary to help. She complained to Jesus, perhaps wanting him to appreciate all that she was doing.

Picture a clergy gathering (or other work setting) at which someone complains about being busy . Others may offer time-saving suggestions or sympathy. The one who has complained feels better now that everyone knows how overworked he or she is.

At one clergy retreat where this common litany of overwork was taking place, the consultant didn't play along. He confronted the complainer, saying, "Something is wrong if you *let* yourself be that overworked. There will always be times when ministers are overly busy. But if your church members *can't* carry on the church programs without consulting you on every decision and having you at every meeting, you'd better do some leadership training. If they *won't* do the work unless you are there, the program probably isn't needed. It's just your program, not theirs." That wasn't really what that overworked minister wanted to hear. He couldn't very well feel like a martyr if it was his own fault he was overworked.

Martha probably didn't want to hear Jesus' response. Note that Jesus didn't criticize Martha's efforts. (Jesus himself often worked long and hard.) Jesus was responding to Martha's unhappiness. He let Martha know it wasn't necessary to do all she was doing.

The text is not about leaving the housework to someone else. Nor does it say it is bad to make fancy preparations for guests—if that brings us pleasure. Neither does it say that spiritual conversation is more important than caring for the needs of others. (Note that this story comes immediately after the story of the Good Samaritan.) It does not insist that the Marthas of the world become like Mary.

The good news needs clear proclamation. It would be sad if the Martha types were to go away from this story with one more "ought" on their list. If serving others is what connects us with God, we can gladly claim that role. When we are burdened by the "oughts" of our lives, we can put the whole list up for review. We can think again about what is really important and can make some room to take care of ourselves by letting go of or simplifying some tasks that are not really life-and-death matters.

Everyone's spiritual needs are different. If we are fed by quiet times of prayer and spiritual reflection, we can claim time to do that. If we are fed by doing things for others or working with our hands, we can claim time to do that. This story is an invitation to pay attention to whatever connects us with God. That is the one thing Jesus knows we all need.

SERMON STARTER: THE LIFE OF THE COMMUNITY

Most commentaries pair the story of Mary and Martha with the story that precedes it, the story of the lawyer who asks Jesus what he must do to inherit eternal life, leading to the parable of the Good Samaritan. These two stories together form an interesting contrast between one who is told to "go and do" and another who is praised for sitting and listening. Both doing and learning are important parts of the Christian life. Then in chapter 11 of Luke, the disciples ask Jesus to teach them to pray. This introduces a group of sayings about prayer that begins with Luke's version of the Lord's Prayer.

Why might the Mary and Martha story be grouped with the section on the Lord's Prayer, rather than with the Good Samaritan? One connection is that Jesus' approval of Mary's decision to sit and learn is followed by a series of Jesus' teachings. A further link between the two stories can be found in the different ways Jesus responded to what Martha asked and what the disciples asked. Martha's request that Jesus tell her sister to help her is rebuffed. The disciples' request that he teach them to pray is rewarded with a sample prayer and a sermon on prayer.

When we explore this latter connection, we can see a contrast between the central vision of Jesus' prayer and the central concern of Martha. Martha was very anxious because she wanted everything to be just right for her guest. Jesus seems not to be at all concerned about whether the hors d'oeuvres are served at the right time. As he has been ever since he stood up in the synagogue in Nazareth and read from Isaiah (Lk. 4:16–21), Jesus is concerned with ushering in the reign of God. The prayer Jesus teaches his disciples is a prayer for the reign of God. So these two passages move from concern for things that do not matter to prayer for the one thing that does matter, that "Your [God's] kingdom come."

Luke's version of this prayer is focused on the coming of God's kingdom. It highlights key elements of life under God's reign. Life under God's reign is life in community. In that community everyone's daily needs are met. Relationships are marked by a willingness to forgive that is rooted in God's forgiveness of us. When the ways of the world clash with the ways of God's community, the world is often violently opposed to the ways of love. Thus, the prayer closes with a petition to be spared from the trials that may come from that clash.

This text could lead to a sermon that explores the current life of the congregation. This can be a prickly subject, so perhaps it could be done with humor that helps the congregation laugh in a gentle way at its own excesses. A story sermon about a mythical congregation could provide enough distance for a congregation to begin to see how it sometimes invests much energy and anxiety in things that do not really matter. Perhaps the story could lift up and celebrate ways a congregation lives and works toward God's reign in its life together in community, even in the midst of distractions with the things that Jesus wouldn't find important.

A different approach might be to explore a current social issue in the local community, nation, or world. The voice of Martha and the words of Jesus' prayer might be used to critique the issue and come to an understanding of what approaches might reflect God's reign among us. One could try to sort out what is not really important and what best creates life-giving community. In such an approach it is important not to leave the congregation with a plate full of "oughts," but to empower action by awakening a yearning for God's present and coming reign.

OFFERING MEDITATION

Mary gave her full attention to Jesus, sitting at his feet to listen to his teaching. Martha also sought to attend to Jesus, but her attention was distracted by her resentment of her sister. Her service, therefore, did not honor Jesus. It was not given in joy and generosity. In all the gifts we give to God, let us give gladly, with attention to what is important.

OFFERING PRAYER

> With these gifts, O God,
>> we celebrate the goodness of life
>> lived in your presence.
> Our hearts are glad to serve you in giving these gifts,
>> in employing these gifts for your work,
>> and in offering our lives for your service.

We pray in the name of the One
   who knows what is important,
   our Savior Jesus Christ. Amen.

COMMUNION MEDITATION

We live in an age of such busyness! Many families sit down together at the table only rarely to eat a meal. Breakfast is grabbed on the run, if at all, as each one races off for a different starting time for work or school. Lunchtime finds most of us away from home. Between sports practice, music lessons, after-school jobs, parents on shift work, and the lure of TV programs, it's hard to find a time when everyone can sit down together for dinner.

In such an age, how are we to understand what it means to gather at Christ's table and eat a meal together? Like Martha, who thought her rushing to and fro to be most important and expected her sister to join her, we may not see the importance of a simple meal shared with loved ones. When we gather with Christ at the table, the feast *is* his presence with us. He is the living bread that satisfies our soul. When we eat together the bread of which he declared, "This is my body," we are drawn together as one body in his name.

In short, when we stop our rushing around and quiet our rushing thoughts and eat and drink this simple meal with Christ and others, we are drawn out of our own agendas and into the community where Jesus Christ defines what is important. First, we are fed and taught by the Word among us. As the Word takes root within us and among us, we can know and choose and do what is important.

Let us gather now at Christ's table for a simple meal together.

BENEDICTION

We have feasted on God's Word and been filled
   with God's vision of the things that matter most.
We are a forgiven people,
   gathered into holy community
   by Christ's presence among us.

May God's love blossom among and within us.
May Christ's vision lead us onward.
May the Spirit shape our life together, now and
    always.
Amen.

John 20:1–18

Sharon Thornton

Alleluia! Christ is risen!
**We come to sing, pray, and shout joyful alleluias,
for Christ is risen today!**
The tomb is empty.
The morning is full.
New life abounds!
Christ is with us! Alleluia! Alleluia!

Opening Prayer

When we saw you on a donkey,
we greeted you with shouts of Hosanna!
While we shared a simple meal with you,
we saw a friend kiss you,
marking your defeat.
When we watched your death
on a cross made of wood,
we left not knowing another day would come.
Then, while we looked the other way,
you called us by our names.
As the sun rises to meet this Easter dawn,
speak our names once more,
that we might be called
to life, to hope, to joy. Amen.

PRAYER OF CONFESSION

Most holy God, we confess that even when we call upon your name, we often feel lost and without hope. Each day the richness of life is all around us, and we often fail to notice. We look away from those who reach out to us, and say we have no friends. We stay in our closed rooms and miss the tender green stalks growing in the rain-soaked soil. We become overwhelmed with bad news and resist the challenges that call for justice. We have failed to halt the violence that still destroys life. We confess our lack of vision that stands in the way of new life.

O God, hold our faltering faith. Deepen our roots in you and move us toward one another. Guide us to Easter hope, that we might live.

Amen.

WORDS OF ASSURANCE

When we confess our sins to God, we will be forgiven. Trust that promise today, knowing it will lead us into a new life of service and joy. Amen.

PRAYERS OF THE PEOPLE

God of life, what you began so long ago you continue in our lives today. You unseal tombs and raise all of life up from the dead. Through your love you unleash hope again in our lives. For this we are truly grateful.

We are grateful and amazed when we see the power of your love reflected in your world today. Our prayers reach out around the world on this Resurrection Day.

We hold before your healing goodness the madness of armed conflict and the threat of wars within and between nations.

We hold before you the travesty of poverty and hunger and the violation of human lives by abuses too dreadful to imagine.

We bring before your cleansing righteousness the growing meanness in the world, staining into the fabric of our lives, spreading across borders, threatening to extinguish flames of goodwill.

We wonder just how it is that your good creation can be so filled with so many kinds of suffering.

We know there are those who cannot feel the joy of this Easter morning. Be with all who bear the burden of depression, those who are worried, those who are visited by grief. Draw close to any who long to hear their names spoken in love, to know the beginning of healing in their lives.

You have created us in the name of love. Make us tender to one another. Incline us toward accepting and forgiving one another that we might begin this marvelous human experiment anew.

May we honor all brave beginnings with a spirit of resurrection joy, especially those that nurture the seeds of justice and compassion in our world.

Call us forth into a sacred partnership with all who glimpse your vision of a renewed creation and believe it possible and worthy.

Restore our broken hearts and set us free from the past.

Move us toward a new day of hope for all.

We are a people of your resurrection promise. Receive the yearnings of our hearts as we open ourselves to you in silence. . .

We ask your Easter blessing in the name of the one who died and rose again and reigns with you still, Jesus Christ our Lord, who taught us when we pray to say: "Our Father…"

CHILDREN'S SERMON: OPPOSITES (BY PATRICIA HATFIELD)

Today we celebrate that although Jesus was once dead, God made him alive again. That's a story we know. We hear it today from John's gospel. The disciples thought the time just after Jesus' death was going to be a very sad day, but it turned out to be the happiest day ever! Today is truly a day of opposites. Listen as I read you a poem by Judy Gattis Smith called "Opposites" (from Judy Gattis Smith, *Birth Death and*

Resurrection: Teaching for Spiritual Growth Through the Church Year [Nashville: Abingdon Press, 1989]).

OPPOSITES

    If things always went *up*
        like balloons from a string,
    But never came *down*
        like a ball to the ground,
    What a strange world it would be.
    If the sun always shone
        and we never had rain,
    If we always were happy
        and never had pain,
    What a strange world it would be.
    If things always were *loud*
        like sirens and screams,
    And never were *quiet*
        like furry shoes seem,
    What a strange world it would be.
    If you always tasted *sharp* things
        like icicles' tips,
    And never drank *smooth* things
        like cool water sips,
    What a strange world it would be.
    If you could only smell roses
        gentle and light,
    And never spicy chili
        on a cold, winter night,
    What a strange world it would be.
    But God had a plan for life to be full
    Of different things—a back and forth pull.
    An up and down swing,
        an in and out prance,
    A high and low fling,
        a round and round dance.
    Listen—oh listen
        to God's secret we hark,
    There always comes daylight
        after the dark.

Once we were sad
>for Jesus was dead.
Today he lives;
>we are singing instead.
What a wonderful world it can be.

Let's pray.

[*Prayer:*] Dear God, thank you for filling the world with opposites: hot and cold, loud and soft, sad and happy. We were very sad when Jesus died, but you showed us how wonderful the world can be when you made Jesus alive again. You are truly a great God! Amen.

SERMON STARTER: EASTER AS HOMECOMING

"Alleluia! Welcome Home!" That's our first greeting to worshipers who appear Easter Sunday. Easter Sunday is homecoming Sunday.

That first Easter morning the impossible became possible, and death crumbled like a day-old rice ball squeezed in the hand of a hungry child. Before a shivering, trembling disciple, out of death came a living, breathing friend. Not a ghost, not a figment of her imagination, but truly the risen Christ.

We are told that on the first day of the week, while it was still dark, Mary Magdalene came to the tomb to prepare Jesus' body for burial. She saw the stone had been moved away from the entrance, and the tomb was empty. Imagine her panic, the pounding of her heart, running, running to find Peter and the other disciple, whom Jesus loved. Breathlessly she spoke: "They have taken the Lord out of the tomb, and we do not know where they have laid him!"

Imagine Peter and the other disciple exchanging a look of horror and then taking off for the tomb. When they arrived, all they saw was burial clothes lying there. The piece of cloth that had covered Jesus' head was rolled up in a place by itself—almost as though it had been ripped off, crumpled, and then flung aside. They knew something extraordinary had happened to Jesus.

Meanwhile, Mary was outside, crying. Her grief was beyond measure. She peered into the tomb and saw two angels in white, one seated at the head and the other at the foot of the place where Jesus' body had lain.

They asked her, "Why are you weeping?" She thought the Roman soldiers, or someone, had come to the tomb and stolen the body of Jesus. (Remember, only a few days earlier she had seen the powerful rulers of the state and the religious establishment savagely turn against her friend.)

Then, as she stood nearby, another voice asked, "Why are you weeping? Whom are you looking for?" She thought he was the gardener.

"Sir, if you have carried him away, tell me where you have laid him, and I will take him away."

Then Jesus said, "Mary!" As if in a dream too good to be true, she turned, recognized him, and spoke: "Rabbouni!"

This story now takes on new and fantastic dimensions. Until now it was unfolding in a predictable way. Jesus was killed on a cross, pronounced dead as the wood he was nailed to, then carried off to a tomb to be buried. Most likely, some crackpot or politician dragged his poor, brutalized body off to conceal the evidence or to prevent any further commotion over this troublesome nobody.

But something else happened along the way. Something unimaginable, something incredible, something right before Mary's eyes. Jesus called Mary's name!

Just when she and the others all thought the grand experiment was a total failure. Friday's events surely proved that. Didn't they?

How startled Mary must have been to see the one she loved, different now, but somehow the same. Her emotions must have been whirling inside her, wanting to believe her eyes and fearing to at the same time. When she heard the sound of her name, Mary knew him.

His voice evoked so many memories. She remembered promises he made to her earlier and possibilities of what might come. And he always told her, "I shall see you again and your heart will rejoice."

Mary trusted that voice, which led her into even deeper levels of faith. For faith is what describes the direction we walk when we find that we are loved. It is what allows us to trust and step out into the unknown with nothing to guide us but a hand just beyond our grasp. Mary rose up out of her sorrow, calling to something deep within herself and larger than her wildest dreams. In those first sunlit hours, it was enough to lift her back into life, holding the words that propelled a whole new movement of Jesus' ministry. She announced, "I have seen the Lord!" and reported what Jesus had said to her.

I cannot tell you anything more than this about what actually occurred on that first Easter morning. But I believe with the faithful of every generation since that somehow Jesus stood there before Mary with the breath of life in him again and the love of God flowing through him.

We gather in this place to celebrate Christ's living presence in and among us, and claim "all is well." Not the Pollyanna sense of closing your eyes to pain and grief. But "all is well" because in the end it is not death that defines our lives. Love defines life, love of such depth and beauty, mystery and blessing, that it is more than any of us have ever dared to dream.

Death crumbled, like a dream forgotten just before waking, and Love emerged. Jesus came to Mary, not like a ghost or a figment of her imagination. And Mary stood up with all the glory of God streaming from her face, her life given back to her in love.

This power of God's resurrection, the power of love, spills over into our lives, where we are called by name and loved. Here is your abiding place: welcome home.

SERMON STARTER: RESURRECTION TESTS THE LIMITS OF CREDIBILITY

Just what do you really believe actually happened that morning when Mary went to the tomb?

Resurrection is not simply remembering the teachings of Jesus.

Resurrection is not simply that Jesus' life is so memorable and vivid that his goodness leaves a trace in his followers' lives like the silver trail of smoke a plane leaves after it vanishes beyond the horizon. Resurrection is not simply a poetic metaphor pointing us to a truth beyond what we can comprehend. Resurrection deepens our understanding of Jesus' teachings, his life, and our human ways of describing him.

But resurrection is more.

It seems to have all begun around dawn. The stone had been rolled away. The body was gone. All four gospels tell the story. Luke says, "Why do you look for the living among the dead? He is not here, but has risen." Matthew says, "Don't be afraid. He is not here; for he has been raised, as he said." Mark says even less and tells them to go look for Jesus in Galilee. The gospel of John simply has Mary announce: "I have seen the Lord."

It would be easier to be a follower of a Jesus who did not rise from the dead. A Jesus who is dead is "fixed"! A dead Jesus wouldn't require anything more. A Jesus who stays dead can simply confirm our suspicions that this life is all there is and that we're to make the best of it. We're born, we marry (or we don't), we grow old, we die. Sometimes we dream of something more, but in the meantime we take comfort in what we know and what we expect. Life is life. Death is the end.

Without the resurrection the story of Jesus would have ended on a God-forsaken hill outside Jerusalem. It would have been just another human tragedy. Unless something very real took place on that "first day of the week," the disciples would have disbanded and we would have heard nothing more.

Easter is *not* a memorial service. The very existence of the New Testament proclaims something different. Something impossible did happen. The disciples were gripped by an experience that transformed them, creating hope in their breaking hearts. The resurrection gave rise to a faith that tells of God's prevailing love in the world. It says that the midnights of this world are still bright enough in the sight of God.

The risen Christ stirs up amazement in us and makes us curious. Perhaps it is foolish that in a world like ours there would be something in us still that says at least "maybe" to this fantastic possibility of God. But the world has never been more disposed to this strange and wonderful word of hope. We are ripe to wonder at all the things that we never think to wonder about because we have become so numb to considering them at all. Because Jesus the Christ somehow got up with life coursing through him again we have this unexplainable confidence that the future can be different.

The resurrection is not a human thing. It belongs to God alone, and so do we.

OFFERING MEDITATION

This Easter day we have seen God's love made flesh. We have heard a voice calling us to life made new.

As we open the walls of our hearts to that good news, may we also open our lives to the needs of the world. Where we can serve face-to-face, let us do so. Where we can help in tangible ways, may we use both grateful hearts and generous spirits to offer our gifts to fill God's world with love.

May these checks and coins serve as signs of our lives, and may our lives become living stones for the building of God's realm of justice and peace, where all can find a home.

OFFERING PRAYER

Accept this offering, O God, and follow it with your blessing. We pray for the day when sharing by all will mean scarcity for none. May our gifts be used toward this glorious end when "all is well." Through you, in you, with you, we live and hope and serve. Amen.

COMMUNION MEDITATION

Resurrection: God's most outlandish sign of generosity! Somehow, the early followers "got it" and began to embody this resurrection generosity in their common life. They knew it was possible to live free of poverty. They willingly became a living example of this. "All who believed were together and had all things in common; they would sell their possessions. . . and distribute the proceeds to all, as any had need" (Acts 2:44–45).

Does anyone still carry this vision today? Anyone strange and wonderful enough who hasn't become completely cynical, who still believes a different world is possible? As we celebrate communion, we lean into God's strange and wonderful future, seeking "the vision of the day when sharing by all will mean scarcity for none" (*Book of Worship* [New York: United Church of Christ, Office of Church Life and Leadership, 1986] 45). Come to the table, where we find life in this common loaf and cup.

—or—

We have offered our gifts. We have said our prayers. We have pondered the scriptures. What more do we need? Perhaps it is something we want so desperately that we can't bring ourselves to ask for it. Maybe what we long for is so outlandish we fear it is foolish to even confess it.

Yet what if Jesus were to come quietly to us—and say our name—as he came to Mary in the garden one quiet morning. Perhaps we long for those eyes of love, the reassurance of a hand placed over ours, something to restore the light in our eyes and the spring that was once in our footsteps.

The early followers of Jesus became encouraged when they came together and shared a common meal. When they broke bread together, the risen Christ became known to them in a special way.

May this be true for us today.

BENEDICTION

> Hold the good news of Easter in your heart.
> Let it work deep into our common life.
> May the One who calls forth new life bless you
>   and fill you with all hope.
> Go out from this worship
>   to embrace the future with courage,
>   and each other in love.
> Christ is risen today!
> **Christ is risen indeed!**
> **Alleluia!**

Acts 10:1–48

Peggy McDonald

SETTING THE SCENE

This text lends itself well to a Sunday when communion is shared. If that is the case, consider having youth bring in chairs at sermon time (a "visual aid") and inviting individuals to come forward to sit in the chairs to receive communion. If communion is not part of the service, help worshipers imagine specific times when they might be the "Peter" or the "Cornelius" of the text. Be as descriptive as possible.

Read the scripture passage from Acts 10 from Eugene Peterson's *The Message: The New Testament, Psalms and Proverbs in Contemporary English* (Colorado Springs: Navpress, 1995). It is lively, informal language and could be read by three or four people, reading the parts of Cornelius, Peter, the others, and the narrator.

CALL TO WORSHIP

God spoke to Cornelius and Peter.
God speaks to us today.
God granted them vision and turned their lives
upside down!
God invites us to look and listen
to discover what it is God will show us today!

OPENING PRAYER

God, you created this world and love it in all its
variety.

We give you thanks for calling together
      this community of believers this morning.
We ask your blessing as we worship you.
Guide our worship,
      that in our prayer, song, and reflection
      we see you more clearly
      and praise you more fully.
Amen.

Prayer of Confession (Unison)

God of mercy, we are not like Peter. We ignore your urging to see the world the way you see it. We harbor prejudices against those who are different from us. We hoard the blessings you've given us, believing we deserve them. We look at those we don't understand with fear, uncertain how to love them the way you do. Forgive us our self-centeredness and narrow-mindedness. Open our eyes to your vision and our hearts to your will. Amen.

Or use God In Between *(see information in the sermon starter below) as inspiration for the prayer of confession, centered around the ways we stumble and fall when we do not see or recognize God in between.*

Words of Assurance

Our God *is* the God of mercy.
**Through the life, death, and resurrection of Jesus
      Christ, we are forgiven!**
Accept God's gift of grace with thanksgiving!

Prayers of the People

Women: God of all, we join in prayer
      to offer you our thanks and praise.
Men: We give you thanks for your Word
      known to us in worship and in our daily lives.
All: **We give you thanks for this community of faith
      and for the church throughout the world.**
Women: We give you thanks for Cornelius and Peter,
      who listened to you and believed you;

Men: for those first followers,
   who had the courage to believe the unbelievable;
All: **and for every person who lives out deep faith.**
Women: Holy God, we ask your blessing
   upon those we name today:
Men: those who lack food and shelter,
All: **those who offer the gift of hospitality,**
Women: innocent victims and children
   who cannot defend themselves,
Men: those whom we take advantage of or ignore,
All: **those who share their bounty**
   for the well-being of others,
Women: the sick and those who grieve,
Men: the unemployed and disenfranchised, and
All: **those known only to you.**
Women: Holy Spirit, open our eyes as you did Peter's.
Men: Grant us the faith that you gave Cornelius.
All: **Form us into the lively and colorful community**
   you would have us be.
Amen.

CHILDREN'S SERMON: NO FAVORITES (BY PATRICIA HATFIELD)

I'd like to know what your favorite ice cream flavor is. (*Get responses to each question.*) What is your favorite color? How about your favorite food? Having a favorite is certainly a good thing. And a yummy thing too!

Sometimes a favorite is not a good thing. Have you ever felt that your brother or sister was your mom or dad's favorite child? How does it make you feel? Which would you rather be, the favorite or not the favorite? How about at school? Do any of you know someone who is the "teacher's pet"? Do you like that the teacher seems to have a favorite student? Do you like the person who is the favorite? Would you want to be the teacher's favorite? (*Allow the children to respond to each question; affirm their responses.*) So sometimes being a favorite is good, and sometimes it is not good.

In our Bible story today, from the New Testament book of Acts, we hear that God does not have favorites. God loves everyone! The Hebrew people thought that God loved only them (they were God's favorite of all the people). People who were not Hebrew were called Gentiles. The Hebrew people *knew* God loved them much, much more than God loved the Gentile people.

Cornelius was a Gentile whose whole family loved God. Cornelius gave money to help the poor, and he prayed every day to God.

At three o'clock one afternoon, Cornelius was saying his prayers. As he prayed, he had a vision (a dream). An angel came to him and said, "Cornelius!" Cornelius was very frightened! The angel said, "Your giving to the poor and your prayers have been noticed by God. Send some men to the city of Joppa to find a man named Peter. Ask him to come and visit you." Immediately Cornelius called three of his men and sent them to Joppa to find Peter.

At noon the next day, Peter went up on the flat roof of his house to wait for lunch. While he waited, he prayed. He, too, had a dream. In Peter's dream he did not see an angel like Cornelius did. Peter saw the sky open and a large sheet come down. In the sheet were all sorts of animals and sea creatures and birds that God's people were not to eat. Then Peter heard a voice saying, "Get up and eat." Peter said, "No! These things are unclean for God's people. I have never eaten anything that God's people may not eat." Then Peter heard the voice say, "Do not call anything unclean that God has made clean." This happened again. And then the same thing happened a third time before the sheet was taken up to the sky.

Peter wondered what the dream meant. What was he to do? As he wondered, the men from Cornelius came and asked for Peter. Peter heard the Holy Spirit say, "Three men have come for you. Go with them because I have sent them." So Peter went down from the roof.

The next day he went to Cornelius' house, where he found a gathering of Cornelius, his family, and friends. Peter saw that Cornelius loved God and helped the poor. And Peter knew God does not have favorites! God loved Peter, and God loved Cornelius and his family. Let's pray.

[*Prayer:*] Dear God, thank you for not having favorites. Thank you for loving each of us the same. Amen.

SERMON STARTER: A COMMUNION SERVICE

These suggestions are for a sermon to be used on a Sunday when communion is served, based particularly on verses 34–36. Focus on all the different kinds of folks that God invites to the table. Below you can find one possibility. Consider which examples would be both provocative and inspiring to your congregation.

Begin by talking about what you do when you invite people over for a gathering. Many hosts make sure guests will have something in common with one another, don't have prejudices against one another, and will easily enjoy themselves. Before guests arrive, the house is cleaned, the table is set, and the furniture pieces are moved to facilitate conversation. Harmony is the key when many people entertain!

Make the sermon visual. Put different kinds of chairs around the table, as if it actually were a table we would sit at for the Lord's supper. Think of the different guests God has invited. Perhaps a nice antique chair where an abolitionist of the nineteenth century would sit. (This scripture passage was used to preach against slavery.) Maybe a kitchen stool for a housewife who organizes marches against abortion. A folding chair for a homeless person. The chair used by the pulpit for a lesbian pastor of a church in another denomination. An executive desk chair for a suited lobbyist. What other kinds of chairs would you include? A Sunday school chair for a child? A wheelchair? This is not the harmonious dinner table imagined above!

Imagine what their conversation would be like. What might they learn from each other about the faith and about themselves?

Invite worshipers to consider who isn't at the table. Who isn't part of your community? Tell a story of a former parishioner, youth of the church, friends, or acquaintances who are disenfranchised from the church or who believe they are not welcome at the table. How did or could you express

Peter's belief, "I truly believe that God shows no partiality" (v. 34)? How can you describe coming to the table through the one who preached peace (v. 36), not division?

Share what good comes from the open invitation of God. Cornelius, C. S. Lewis, and individuals you know have come to the faith because it is passed on through the work of the Holy Spirit. Many of us come to the faith through our families of origin, but not all of us do! Describe how the life of the church or your life is richer because of people new to the faith (e.g., someone from another church where you were a member, a fellow pastor who converted to Christianity as an adult). The gifts we receive individually include faith, a new understanding of each other, a group with which to share our gifts and talents (which causes them to multiply), a community to nurture us as we each grow in wisdom and stature. The greatest gift of all is that God is glorified as the church multiplies, expands, and changes.

Close the sermon by adding a chair to the table and inviting the congregation to prepare in their hearts for the celebration of communion by inviting "Cornelius" to join in at the feast.

SERMON STARTER: A CHILDREN'S BOOK

Base your sermon on the children's book by Sandy Sasso, *God In Between*. It is the story of a town of people who couldn't see God and had no community life because of it. Once they realize that God is in between them, they put windows in their houses and build streets and sidewalks. Because they can see, they can be a community (Sandy Sasso, *God In Between*, Jewish Lights Publishing, Sunset Farm Offices, Rte. 4, P.O. Box 237, Woodstock, VT 05091; 802-457-4000).

Speak directly to the specific concerns within your congregation. Address a particular place in which community has been established despite typical hesitations or prejudices. Find a way to affirm the congregation for action taken in an earlier time (perhaps opening the door to persons from another country, another race, another economic strata).

Hypothesize what might happen if this congregation were to add a new "window." Tell a story of another situation where that same "window" was added, and the congregation grew deeper in faith, broader in understanding, or greater in numbers because of the risk.

Reflect upon a passage from *Amazing Grace* by Kathleen Norris, from the chapter called "Intolerance/Forbearance," pages 158–60:

> The polarization that characterizes so much of American life is risky business in a church congregation, but especially so in a monastic community. The person you're quick to label and dismiss as a racist, a homophobe, a queer, an anti-Semite, a misogynist, a bigoted conservative or a bleeding-heart liberal is also a person you're committed to live, work, pray and dine with for the rest of your life…How do they do it? They know, as one Anglican nun has put it, that their primary ministry is prayer, and that prayer transcends theological differences. They also have the wisdom of St. Benedict, "They should each try to be the first to show respect to the other"…A Trappist abbot recently told me about a psychologist who had conducted a weeklong retreat for his community, during which monks of all ages had gone to the visitor to talk about their lives. After a few days the man came to the abbot and said: "I thought the age of miracles was past! How in the world can these people stand to live together for one day, let alone for years?" The abbot responded, "I've never been able to figure it out. And I'm afraid to ask." I respect that abbot's humility, the good sense he has to leave a mystery alone and accept it with gratitude. (Kathleen Norris, *Amazing Grace, A Vocabulary of Faith* [New York: Riverhead Books, 1998])

As appropriate, use this as the opportunity to challenge the congregation to a particular action. Where might you find God "in between" if this action were taken?

If communion follows the sermon, invite worshipers to look carefully for God in between themselves and those with whom they kneel (or those to whom they pass the communion elements).

OFFERING PRAYER

> Almighty God, you ask us to make a place in our lives
> for you as well as for strangers.

Accept these gifts as signs of our thankful response.
Here we give for the mission of this congregation
and our mission in the world.
Here we renew our commitment
to see your reflection
in the strangers we meet.
Through your Spirit, allow us to see
every person with your eyes.
Following our Savior, Jesus Christ,
guide us as we walk with those
who most need to meet you.
We pray in the name of the one who showed the
world your gracious love, Jesus Christ.
Amen.

COMMUNION MEDITATION

The Holy Spirit nudged Cornelius and said, "Your
prayer has been heard. Find Peter!"
And the Spirit hurried to Peter's room and said, "Go
to the door. Speak with your guests. You have
been waiting for them."
The bread is baked, the wine poured,
and the gracious host, Jesus Christ, has invited
all—Cornelius, Peter, even you and me!
Come, share the meal that has been set before you.
Accept the faith, live in the grace,
and tell the story of this gift you have received.

OFFERING MEDITATION (COULD BE DONE IN UNISON)

Adults: Like Cornelius, our hearts are open.
Children: Like Peter, our minds are racing.
Adults: Our hands are eager.
Children: We want to thank God!
**All: We return to God the gifts we have received!
Amen.**

BENEDICTION (COULD BE IN TWO VOICES OR SOLO)

Go out into the world in hope
to witness to the power of the One who created us.

Go out into the world in love
> **to nurture the ones who long to know Christ's friendship.**

Go out into the world in peace
> **to celebrate the diversity of the family of faith.**

Alleluia! Amen.

Revelation 21:1–7

Laura Loving

This service lifts up the image of the holy city and leans toward the inbreaking of God's hopes for the world. Here the hopeful image of the holy city envisioned by God blooms and challenges worshipers to find a way to go through the time warp of already/not yet.

Call to Worship

God, who is with us from beginning to end,
    calls us to this time of worship.
God, who is the Alpha and the Omega,
    loves us completely.
We begin our service with songs of praise and
    adoration.
Holy, Holy, Holy God!
Heaven and Earth are full of your glory.
Let us worship the God who is both
exalted and present, constant and changing,
    at home with us and yet awesome to behold.
Alleluia!

Opening Prayer

O God, you have made your home in our midst, yet your mystery sometimes clouds our understanding of who you are. Make yourself known to us in this hour. Breathe your hopes and dreams into us. Call us your own. Draw us into your dream for a new world, a new way, a new day, for we long to be your people and to live out your hopes. We pray in the name of Jesus, who is our hope and our home. Amen.

PRAYER OF CONFESSION (UNISON)

> **God, you have dreamed of a holy city.**
> **Yet we have created cities scarred**
> > **by scarcity and sorrow.**
> **Our children are hungry and poorly housed.**
> **Our young men and women have nightmares**
> > **instead of dreams.**
> **Our air is swirling with words of hate,**
> > **with clouds of pollution,**
> > **with winds of distrust.**
> **Revive our hopes for our cities.**
> **Stir us with compassion to care for your children,**
> > **our children, and the children of others.**
> **Restore in our youth the dreams of the future**
> > **that carry them forward**
> > **with excitement and hope.**
> **Clear our eyes to see the importance**
> > **of the words we speak, the air we breathe,**
> > **and the trust we build**
> > **among our brothers and sisters.**
> **We have fallen short of your dreams for us.**
> **In your mercy, lift us and give us new life,**
> > **in Jesus Christ our Lord. Amen.**

WORDS OF ASSURANCE

> God is merciful and just, forgiving our sin
> > and bringing us new life.
> **God will wipe away our tears**
> > **and wipe the slate clean.**
> In Jesus Christ,
> > God's grace is made real and revealed to us.
> **Thanks be to God for the gift of grace!**

PRAYER OF THE PEOPLE

> O Well of Hope, you have promised
> > to give water to the thirsty,
> > and so we turn to you in prayer.

We are longing to be refreshed by your presence.
We bear the burden
 of trying to carry the world on our shoulders.
Help us to remember that it is not ours alone.
We thirst for knowledge
 and are drowning in information.
Grant us wisdom and discernment
 to enrich the life of our minds.
We give you thanks for the richness of life,
 for vibrant cities that pulse
  with life and excitement,
 for rich farmland and craggy mountains,
 for deep lakes and mighty rivers,
 for the taste of oranges and the color of rain.
All your good gifts remind us
 that the burden of life is balanced
  by the mystery of life.
So make us your faithful, constant people.
Steady us lest we give up hope too easily.
Remind us to look for the face of Christ
 in stranger and sojourner, family and friend.
Help us to find comfort there.
Thank you for this vision of hope
 that pulls us forward,
 that dawns each day,
 and that settles into our consciousness at night.
O Well of Hope,
 deep is our gratitude, long is our prayer,
 drenched in goodness, we are yours. Amen.

CHILDREN'S SERMON: NO MORE TEARS (BY PATRICIA HATFIELD)

Why do people cry? Different people cry for different reasons. Like babies. Why do you think babies cry? (*Because they are hungry; they need their diapers changed; they don't know how to talk.*) What about grown-ups? Grown-ups cry too. Why do you think grown-ups cry? (*Because they are sad about a death or a sad movie, or because they are happy at a wedding or other special occasion.*) It sounds like grown-ups cry for a lot of different reasons too. So what about kids? What makes kids cry? (*Because they are sad or angry; because they have lost something or they have become lost; because they are hurt or injured. Allow plenty of time.*)

What do your mom and dad do when they see you crying? (*They hug you, kiss you, say things to help you.*) How does that make you feel? Have you ever comforted someone who was crying? What did you do? (*Again, allow ample time for the children to respond.*)

God is surely happy when there are people to comfort you when you are crying. God is surely happy when you comfort other people who are crying.

In our Bible story this morning, we hear about a time when there will be a new heaven and a new earth. The new Jerusalem (part of the new earth) is described as a beautiful city...as beautiful as a bride in her long white wedding gown, with a beautiful bouquet of flowers. And God will live with us, right next door to us! Best of all, God says there will be no more tears. There will be no death, no sadness, and no pain. God will wipe away all our tears. We don't know when God will make this new earth. But it gives us hope that there will not always be tears. And until then, we can wipe away each other's tears, just as God plans to do when the new earth comes. Let's pray.

[*Prayer:*] Dear God, thank you for special people in our lives who can wipe away our tears: our moms and dads, our friends, and our loved ones. We thank you that we can help wipe away the tears of others. And we pray, God, that you will make the new earth very, very soon so that people will not have to cry ever again. Amen.

SERMON STARTER: THE HOLY CITY

A series of possibilities:

Address the contrasts and similarities between the city as seen by John and the city as we perceive it today.

Focus on inspiring people to recommit to work toward justice, safety, diversity, and holiness in the city.

Hold up imagery from this passage. Suggest concrete ways the congregation might get involved in or celebrate ministry: working with Habitat for Humanity; tutoring or providing after-school space for young people; forming a legislative monitoring group that tracks the progress and roadblocks to creating strong and healthy cities; getting involved in a shelter or meals program; or making the life of the city a constant on the church's prayer chain.

Encourage people to match the dreamlike language of Revelation with concrete suggestions that pertain to your community.

Why is it that the vision of the holy city eludes us generation after generation? We get so close! We create communities rich in diversity, full of industry, teeming with life and music and possibility. But underneath, the families living in the sewers and the subways are a reminder that the holy is not wholly here.

Underneath, the crumbling roads and halting bridges between races and classes and genders and cultures remind us we have created these cities in our image, not in the image of God. We have built them with our selfishness, our love of power, our shortsightedness.

Stop and listen to the imagery of the book of Revelation.

What would it be like to create the holy city
    in our midst?
    With God's help.
    In God's time.
    In God's image.
It would mean letting go even as we are building.
It would mean emptying even as we are landfilling.
It would mean humility and tears and fresh ideas
    and listening to one another
    and honoring instead of tolerating.
What would it mean for you,
    in your own town, your own city,
    your own family, your own community?
What would it mean for you to receive
    God's fresh vision of the holy city?

SERMON STARTER: PARADOX

A series of possibilities:

Deal with the familiar and yet elusive quality of the language in this passage.

Finally, the vision of chapter 21 appears, and with it comes familiar language that is welcome to the weary navigator: the new Jerusalem, the dwelling of God with God's people, the end of death and of grief. The sense of the familiar is ironic, of course; while the language and the promises are familiar, this new creation is no less a promise yet to be fulfilled than when it was written in the late first century. (Walter Brueggemann, et al., *Texts for Preaching: A Lectionary Commentary Based on the NRSV—Year B* [Louisville: Westminster/John Knox Press, 1993], 608–9)

Navigate through the shoals of a concept of time that is paradoxical, prophetic, visionary, and startling to the linear, left-brained congregants and people who think in literal images. It's a paradox that calls us into a deeper understanding of how God is both Alpha and Omega, imminent and transcendent.

Look at the signs of hope in the world around your church. Investigate the world through this lens of possibility, encouraging daily mindfulness, the surrender to paradox, and the challenge to live as fragments of God's vision in the world today.

Question what it means to declare: "God's home is among mortals" (v. 3). Portray God as a homemaker among us, one who offers hospitality, nurtures our hopes, wipes away our tears, and comforts us in pain. This intimate portrait of God could be a springboard for a pastoral sermon about the presence of God. Think about the situations facing the congregation: divorce, living with chronic illness, celebrating a new sense of vocation, adjusting to retirement, mourning the loss of a loved one, facing the challenge of caring both for frail parents and active children, dealing with the injustices of racism, classism, sexism—from either side. Use these situations to explore how God as homemaker might make us feel more at home in our own skin. This could be done in a dialogue format, as the Holy Homemaker engages the folks in these life situations, or as a monologue as God sips tea at the end of the day. Use the creativity engendered in this apocalyptic writing to season your sermon.

One of the toughest "sells" in the life of faith is the preponderance of paradoxes. We are living in the already/not yet. Our God is the Alpha and the Omega. We are called to be servants, yet empowered by the greatest force in the universe. We are to be humble, yet boasting of the gospel. The Ancient One makes all things new.

Living with the paradoxes of faith helps us to step away from rational, all-or-nothing thinking. It defies the proof-texting, recipe-following approach to faith. It requires that we use our God-given imagination to hold the paradox in creative tension.

How does this paradoxical approach to life affect your daily life?

What does it say about your particular vocation?

Will you dare to live in that fragile, steel-strong place of faith?

If so, you may be on to something.

OFFERING MEDITATION

God has offered us a vision of hope. What can we offer in return? We offer the symbols of our labor, the work of city, farm, school, factory. We offer our gifts with love and thanksgiving and harbor here the hope that the realm of God, the holy city, will be built brick by brick, with the compassionate and caring sacrifice of the people of God.

PRAYER OF DEDICATION

Here are our gifts, O God. They came from you; they belong to you. Use them to design the blueprints of that place where crying ceases, justice rules supreme, and hunger and thirst are no more. Use us and the ministry of this church to bring in your realm, in Christ's name and for the sake of the world. Amen.

COMMUNION MEDITATION

"God will wipe away every tear."

"Death shall be no more."

These promises from the apocalyptic book of Revelation (echoing the prophet Isaiah) are bold affirmations of faith.

We come to the table, making these same bold affirmations. Here, our tears our wiped away by the One who is our Host. Here, death is conquered as we remember Christ's dying and rising. The victory over suffering is complete. The dreamlike quality of the banquet draws us in. As we sit at the table with saints and sinners of all generations, time is eclipsed, love is triumphant, death is no more. Pour out your sorrows and joy and receive the fullness of God in Jesus Christ. Amen.

BENEDICTION

Go from this place, inspired by the vision of God.

Lift high the banner of hope, leaning into the day when there is no thirst, no hunger, no death, no tears, but only the glorious city of God, the new Jerusalem.

May God give us boldness and courage to follow the dream.

May God, the Alpha and the Omega, be with you from the beginning to the end.

Amen.

Music Suggestions: Hymns and Anthems

Bill Thomas

Hymns and anthems are an integral part of every worship service. For ease of reference, suggestions for hymns and anthems are cataloged by the service for which they are intended rather than incorporated into the material for the service.

For each service, five hymns are suggested. They come in order:

- Opening Hymn (or Hymn of Praise)
- Prayer Hymn
- Hymn of Commitment (hymn following the sermon)
- Communion Hymn
- Closing Hymn

They can almost all be found in *Chalice Hymnal* (St. Louis: Chalice Press, 1995). Where possible, the same hymn is designated from the Methodist, Presbyterian, and United Church of Christ hymnals.

For each service, one or more choral anthems are suggested. Most of them are available from:

Pepper Church Music Co.
Phone: 1-800-345-6296
Fax: 1-800-260-1482
Internet: www.jwpepper.com

The catalog numbers appear after each selection. All of the catalog numbers listed are for SATB arrangements. For two- or three-part arrangements of the same anthem, the inventory number will be slightly different. Pepper will look that up for you over the phone or will send you a catalog with that information.

"In the Beginning" must be obtained from Harold Flammer, Inc.

"He Restoreth My Soul" can be found in specialty music stores that carry African-American or gospel sheet music.

Hymn Suggestions

Scripture & Hymn Name	Chalice Hymnal	Methodist	Presbyterian	United Church of Christ
Genesis 1:1—2:4a				
Let's Sing Unto the Lord	60	149		
Restless Weaver	658			
All Creatures of our God and King	22	62	455	17
Seed, Scattered and Sown	395			
When in Awe of God's Creation	688			
Exodus 3:1–12				
If You Will Trust in God	565		282	410
Lead Me, Guide Me	583			
Here I Am, Lord	452	593	525	
I Hunger and I Thirst	409			
Lead On, O Cloud of Presence	633			
1 Samuel 16:1–13				
Holy Wisdom	258			
Spirit of the Living God	259	393	322	283
O God of Vision	288			
Take our Bread	413			
God the Spirit, Guide and Guardian	450	648	523	355
Psalm 23				
God Is My Shepherd	79			479
He Leadeth Me, O Blessed Thought	545	128		
How Firm a Foundation	618	529	361	407
All Who Hunger, Gather Gladly	419			
How Great Thou Art	33	77	467	
Psalm 150				
Praise to the Lord, the Almighty	25	13		
For Each Day	605			
All Creatures of Our God and King	22	62	455	17
Give Thanks	528			
Let the Whole Creation Cry	21		256	

Scripture & Hymn Name	Chalice Hymnal	Methodist	Presbyterian	United Church of Christ
Isaiah 11:6–9				
All Earth Is Waiting	139	210		121
Emmanuel, Emmanuel	134	204		
People Look East	142	202	12	
O God Unseen, Yet Ever Near	399			
Come, Thou Fount	16	400	356	459
Matthew 1:18–25				
Her Baby Newly Breathing	158			
Infant Holy, Infant Lowly	163	229	37	
Sing of God Made Manifest	176			
I Wonder as I Wander	161			
Go Tell It On the Mountain	167	251	29	154
Mark 1:1–15				
What Was Your Vow and Vision	177			
Forty Days and Forty Nights	179			205
Jesus Saves!	479			
Jesus Walked This Lonesome Valley	211			
Go My Children With My Blessing	431			82
Luke 10:38—11:4				
Take Time to Be Holy	572	395		
The Lord's Prayer	307	271	589	
Open My Eyes, That I May See	586	454	324	
Jesus, Keep Me Near the Cross	587	301		197
Wellspring of Wisdom	596	506		
John 20:1–18				
I am the Light of the World	469			584
Savior Like a Shepherd Lead Us	558	381	387	252
All Hail the Power	92	154	143 (Diadem preferred)	304
We Meet You, O Christ	183	257	387	
Transform Us	182			
He Lives!	226	310		
Acts 10:1–48				
O For a World	683			575
Somos Uno en Christo	493			
Siyahamba!	442			526
Diverse in Culture, Nation, Race	485			
O God We Bear the Imprint	681			
Revelation 21:1–7				
O Day of God Draw Nigh	700	730	450	
O Day of Peace That Dimly Shines	711	729	450	
When All Is Ended	703			
A Hymn of Joy We Sing	404			
My Eyes Have Seen the Coming				610

Anthem Suggestions

Genesis 1:1—2:4a	In the Beginning—Willy Richter, Flammer Inc. or O Sifuni Mungu—1914175
Exodus 3:1–12	Lead Me to the Rock—Wilkinson/Morton 313798-420 or Led by the Spirit—C. Berry 3124690-420
1 Samuel 16:1–13	The Lord Desires These Things—3147949-420 or Change my Heart/Lord Be Glorified—3092392-420
Psalm 23	He Restoreth My Soul—arr. A.E. Williams or The King of Love My Shepherd Is or Savior, Like a Shepherd Lead Us—3147808
Psalm 150	Praise to the Lord—3137593 or Canticle of Praise—John Ness Beck
Isaiah 11:6–9	And the Glory of the Lord (Messiah) or Every Valley—Beck 1200971-420 (SATB)
Matthew 1:18–25	African Noel—30843357-423 or Come See the Baby—3071297-420
Mark 1:1–15	O Master Let Me Walk With Thee—3074747 or Savior Like a Shepherd, Lead Us—3147808 or I Want Jesus to Walk With Me—3073731
Luke 10:38—11:4	'Tis So Sweet to Trust in Jesus—3108032 or Be Thou My Vision—3151180 or Make Me a Channel of Your Peace
John 20:1–18	He is Alive—3134418 or Worthy is the Lamb/Amen Chorus (Messiah) or Easter Celebration—3108453
Acts 10:1–48	In Christ There Is No East Or West—John Ness Beck or The Family of God—Mark Hayes
Revelation 21:1–7	The Holy City—773465 or When I Get to Heaven, I Will Sing—3111788

List of BIBLE QUEST Scriptures

This book of worship resources may be used on its own or in coordination with the BIBLE QUEST curriculum for congregations. If you are using BIBLE QUEST curriculum for September 2000 through August 2001, the theme of incarnation contains twelve bookmark stories. This list shows the bookmark stories for each month in the first year of BIBLE QUEST. All these scriptures are included in this book.

September 2000	Genesis 1:1—2:4a
October 2000	Exodus 3:1–12
November 2000	1 Samuel 16:1–13
December 2000	Isaiah 11:6–9
January 2001	Matthew 1:18–25
February 2001	Mark 1:1–15
March 2001	Acts 10:1–48
April 2001	John 20:1–18
May 2001	Revelation 21:1–7
June 2001	Psalm 150
July 2001	Psalm 23
August 2001	Luke 10:38—11:4